TRANSCENDING RELATIONSHIPS

ON THE ENLIGHTENED PATH

SCOTT E. CLARK

Bodhi Publishing Company, LLC
Phoenix, Arizona, USA

Library of Congress Control Number: 2016906002
Tradepaper ISBN: 978-0-9903198-2-5
1st printing, March 2016
Printed in the United States of America Copyright

WITH GRATITUDE

I offer my appreciation for all of the many teachers I have had within this human experience. Each of you has played a role in shaping my present reality and level of consciousness, leading to the message in this book series. I also express my gratitude to all people who are endeavoring to live enlightened. The world needs your light in whatever unique form or method you have been gifted to provide it.

I forever acknowledge my greatest legacy and most joyous blessing as my children, grandchildren, and family. You have giving me purpose and support in the darkest of hours. And you make the daily journey most rewarding.

Thank you to Etana Holowinko (www.livesocietyjazz.com) for your talent and inspiration in the design of the cover, and for other technical and artistic contributions. I also wish to acknowledge Chelle Thompson (www.inspirationline.com) for her wonderful editing services. And finally, I would like to show appreciation to the great contemporary teachers of higher truth who inspire us to greater love, peace and unity.

TABLE OF CONTENTS

INTRODUCTION

"Don't ask yourself what the world needs, ask yourself what makes you come alive. And then go and do that. Because what the world needs are people that are alive."

- Howard Thurman

Welcome to *On the Enlightened Path*. In this series, each book is designed to bring an "Awakened" perspective to the various essential aspects of your human experience. As the title indicates, this book addresses the very powerful process of **TRANSCENDING RELATIONSHIPS**.

Within this aspect of our life we will know the highest joys and the deepest sorrows. This encompasses beginnings, like the birth of our children or a new love affair, to endings, such as divorce or death, and everything in between. While our life is something for us to behold, our lessons largely play out within the form of relationship.

Relationships are a very significant part of our human experience which, I realize, sounds like an obvious statement. However, do you fully understand the true meaning and power of your relationships? The ones that feel good and those that don't, both the long-term and the briefest relations. Do you know that they are not as random or coincidental as they may seem? Are you able to utilize your relationships in support of your healing, growth, and evolution? And are you able to realize your greatest self-love and inner strength as you create and maintain relationships that support your empowerment and wellness? These questions and more will be addressed within the content of this book.

1

I myself have utilized the many and varied life experiences and lessons presented to me in relationships for my own transformation, healing, and growth. And I know that this is always ongoing. I have certainly been required to experience my share of volatility in the past. Yet, I now understand that this was my path and process of learning to know and honor my truth. As I now apply the principles of self-mastery and higher consciousness in my life, I am fulfilling my human connections within a higher energetic state. This becomes more supportive of me and all others involved.

Through our expressions of energy we create all of our experiences, including our relationships. When we can do this more consciously and intentionally we will realize the greatest reward and fulfillment. I considered using the word "Loving" in the title, but I wanted to be clear that this wisdom pertains to all of our human relationships. And using the "L" word may mislead some to think that this is merely about our intimate partner relations.

Transcending means "going above and beyond the limits of ordinary experiences," to realize something "far better or greater than the usual." Therefore, transcending relationships represents an understanding and awareness that honors your own inner truth and leads to your greatest wellness and fulfillment. It requires and empowers us to be fully accountable in our choices and expressions of energy. As we elevate our consciousness in this area, we will more naturally seek to be supportive of the well-being of all others as well.

Within every segment of our life we have been impacted by our relations with other people. Through these experiences we have accumulated many energetic impressions (thoughts and feelings) that have come to define our self-image. We have attracted our relationships in order to learn, heal, and develop ourselves as we pursue our best life. But did we learn our higher truth, or did we simply accept and absorb some negativity that then became limiting and disempowering in some way?

2

The quality of the alignment to our truth, versus our ego attachment, will determine the level of success and fulfillment we will recognize in our lives. Were we able to identify an opportunity to choose self-love and empowerment from the experience, or did we give away our power and give in to our fear? Our previous associations have led us to not only define ourselves, but our perceptions of the world around us as well. On our path we have felt every type of emotion, from elation to depression, as we have shared our energy with others.

An awakened view of our relationships supports us in clearly determining the effect that our interactions with another have on our energy, and therefore our wellness. We may use our awareness to determine, "is this experience (or memory) elevating or depleting us?" And then, "what is it that we can do to be more empowered and transcendent in this moment?"

Are you a slave to your current or past relationship experiences, or are you a master? The first book in this series, *Mastering Your Life*, teaches that you are here to be the master of your unique and intentional life. This is a most powerful truth within the most powerful tool you will have in this life for healing, growth, and ascension – your Relationships!

Our relationships offer great value in both our spirituality and our humanity. There is a dual purpose – practical functioning in the material world, and energetic healing and fulfillment to the Soul. We will necessarily encounter all types of relationships in order to make our way through this human journey. Therefore, this book brings an enlightened view of our family relationships and upbringing, our intimate relationships, friendships and other human connections, and even our isolated space between certain relationships. We have had many beginnings and endings, joys and frustrations (or worse). And while this can be hard to accept within our space of disempowerment, the truth is that we have attracted all of this in support of our own well-being.

The key, as I will express in depth throughout this book, is to utilize the tool of relationships in an enlightened manner.

Through higher wisdom you can learn to understand the full dynamic of your relationships. Then you may shift your perceptions and intentions for the greatest fulfillment and success, according to your truth. As always, the goal is to integrate your Authentic Self into your human experiences – this is enlightened living.

How you interact with others, and then process these experiences within yourself, is immensely valuable to your quality of life and evolution. We must develop ourselves to be fully awake and conscious in how we choose, and then maintain, all of our relationships. Otherwise, to be unconscious, is allowing others to dictate their terms and agenda to us. I am sure you will concur that this is very disempowering and unsatisfying.

This is not about being more forceful, aggressive, or dominating, as a way to get what you want. Your greatest power comes when in alignment with the loving energy of your higher identity, in understanding your own truth and living within the inner strength to honor yourself. Our relationships provide continual tests which will determine our level of self-love. This requires a more sincere devotion to your own healing, growth, and well-being. And therefore, relationships provide a wonderful spiritual practice.

As always, the enlightened path requires accountability. As you work to shine the light of truth upon your own life and path, you improve the quality of your human experiences. And then, with this more empowering focus, you may express your loving presence for greater love, peace, joy, and compassion with others.

Within my own spiritual practice, I have allowed my higher guidance to show me the truth about my past relationships as a tool for transformation and greater love, understanding, and evolution. However, like most people, there were times of great struggle when I was not seeing or accepting the truth I was being taught. As long as we are unwilling or unable to accept our complete accountability for attracting and creating our relationships, we will suffer from the ego-delusion that is quick to blame others.

I have experienced most every type of relationship and breakup. I have been married and divorced more than once, have had many friends come and go, and experienced the innumerable family and co-worker relationship situations. For me there have been many beginnings and endings. And where I previously thought this was a problem, I now recognize it as serving a great purpose in my unique life path. This has been my process of inner development, leading to the fulfillment of my Soul's purpose.

In the writing of this book I have utilized the lessons in wisdom that have shifted my understanding and consciousness in the area of relationships. I have also invoked the power of a present moment connection to Divinity in support of the teaching that I have been guided to share on this topic.

Within the format of this book, I am taking a 3-Part approach to intentionally creating *Transcending Relationships*. This process is designed to offer information and inspiration that will help you in the following ways:

Part I) Realizing a Higher Truth – Guides you toward an understanding and recognition of the higher purpose and value in all of your relationships.

Part II) Learning and Healing from the Past – Teaches you the wisdom that supports you in shifting to a greater acceptance of the past and place of wellness in the present.

Part III) Offer Your Loving Presence to Others – Coaches you to utilize the higher wisdom and healing from Parts 1 and 2, toward creating more empowering and fulfilling relationships in the present.

Your highest capacity within this human experience is to live enlightened. This is an internal connection to your Divinity, which then may be applied to all areas of life. When experiencing your relationships from this healthy awakened space, you will elevate your energy from a preponderance of fearful expressions (thoughts, feelings, words, and actions) to a much greater connection to the Divine energy of love. You will literally shift the way in which you see yourself and the world around you. Your reality will expand.

As you begin to live more awakened and transcendent, you may reflect the light of your truth into all of your current associations and interactions. They will continue to be a source of learning and growth for you. But they are also an opportunity to fulfill your higher purpose, support the well-being of others, and to embrace and promote unity consciousness. May this teaching bless you within all aspect of your life, and especially your relationships with all others.

Namaste!

THE AWAKENED PATH OF ENLIGHTENMENT

"You are not a human being in search of a spiritual experience. You are a spiritual being immersed in a human experience."

- Pierre Teilhard de Chardin

The above quote states a key concept that opens many doors toward empowering you to shift to a new, higher perspective of your life, and thereby expand your opportunities for healing, growth, wellness, and success. You are a spiritual being having a human experience, and not the other way around. Therefore, when you reside in your truth you are more than your human problems, challenges, and falsely limited self-perception.

A term that is critical to personal and spiritual growth is "consciousness." To me, consciousness is a force that connects our humanity to our Divinity. When this is weak or slight, our connection to Spirit (love, truth) is also weak, while our attachment to our humanity (ego) is strong. As we elevate level of consciousness in the present moment, we strengthen our connection to our Divinity, and release the hold of our ego. This then supports a transformational shift to a higher perspective of our identity, purpose, potential, etc.

This shift to higher consciousness does not take anything away from your humanity. Instead, it supports you toward greater power and accountability to live your best life while human. You are literally authorized by your very nature to create a life based in love, empowerment, and purpose, regardless of what you or anyone else may have thought about you in the past.

You came into this world to live and experience your own unique life path, as part of an even more expansive Soul journey. You are the **MASTER** of your life, and uniquely qualified to create the experiences and conditions that are most rewarding within the context of your higher purpose. Therefore, endeavor to determine and then live from the place of your truth.

The first key factor in **Mastering Your Life** (the first book in the *"On the Enlightened Path"* series) is to realize your Authentic Self within this human experience. Our Authentic Self represents two things. First, it is your highest nature as Divine energy (a spiritual being). You are an individuation of Divine Source (Universal Intelligence, God, or whatever name you prefer), a Soul or Spirit that is both its own distinct entity and at the same time connected to all that is.

This is significant to our humanity in that, as a part of Divinity, we have access to all of the qualities of Divinity. These include love, peace, joy, creativity, wellness, compassion, abundance, etc., which represent the qualities we all most desire to experience within our humanity. Conversely, these qualities are not sustainable while controlled by ego. However, for the purpose of functioning separately in this human experience, we have adopted the condition of free will. So it is for us to intentionally "awaken" and choose our higher identity, qualities, and possibilities within this human existence.

The second realization about our Authentic Self is that regarding our own life path as human, we have all that we need in order to fulfill our Divine purpose. It is for us to choose to honor our own unique gifts, qualities, circumstances, and passions, and then transcend and transform within the context of our life. Not all human lives offer the same opportunities for material things like, financial wealth, popularity, optimal physical health, position of power, etc. Yet, from wherever we are, we CAN improve our lives by elevating our consciousness and experiencing the higher Divine qualities available to us.

As we can understand and accept our true higher connection and identity, we will realize more joy, empowerment, and success in living our best life. Previously, we may have lived within the perception that we were lacking or disadvantaged, and therefore, unable to find satisfaction or fulfillment. We had been overly focused on the comparison to, and input from, other people. Through higher wisdom we now know that we can shift our focus toward appreciating that which we do have, and then further develop our gifts in order to enhance our love, joy, peace, abundance, and wellness.

The second key to a **Mastering Your Life** is to claim the power of the present moment. Within this key we will endeavor to develop and maintain our greatest awareness, mindfulness, and Presence. In doing so, we make the most empowering choices for our lives while connected to the only moment that exists – the present moment. In truth, this also represents the only time in which we are connected to our Divine Nature. The past is gone, nothing can change it; and the future is a distant present moment yet to be lived. Only your mind and ego exist in these places, and not your Spirit.

While we are conscious (connected with awareness to Divine Presence) we may live in the present, utilizing our highest qualities. We can choose to offer love to ourselves and others, for whatever external condition exists. With our full focus and mindfulness in reality we may create space apart from the delusions of ego. This leads us to greater production and fulfillment within any aspect of our lives. I find this to be a satisfying definition of success!

When we go "unconscious," we lose our mind to delusion; this is where fear steps in and takes control. There may be countless memories from past experiences that consume our mind, and usually we only ruminate over the negative mental images. Or we live our current circumstances within the framework of unhealed past perceptions. Why did that happen? What did I do wrong? Why did they treat me that way? And fear then brings the emotions connected to it, like: anger, sadness, resentment, judgement, blame, shame, lack, victimhood, greed, etc. Or we get lost in our anxiety about the future based upon the situations and perceptions in which we are unsatisfied with in the present.

This encompasses the typical mental patterns of the unattended mind – one that lacks the quality of mindfulness. As a part of living enlightened we must develop greater awareness and discipline with our minds in order to create the more positive experiences we desire. Otherwise, our lack of wisdom and understanding of our true capabilities, along with a lack of accountability, will doom us. This causes us to create needless suffering in our own lives.

Noticing where we are in our minds, as well as our level of energy, becomes our greatest spiritual practice. This not only reveals our thoughts but also the quality of our energy. And of course, all things (ourselves included) are made up of energy. So we want to recognize whether we are investing in fear or love; and then, when necessary, re-align our energy to the higher qualities of love. This is how we live more often within the energetic space of peace, joy, kindness, gratitude, abundance, compassion, wellness, etc.

This represents the ongoing path and nature of enlightenment. You are never there, you are always in process. The conditions of inner healing and growth require us to be mindful and present, as we intentionally become responsible for our own wellness. It seems that many people are quite challenged in living their awakened higher path. It would be easier if some guru or other outside source could just come along and make you instantly "enlightened." But it doesn't work that way; your Soul has its own destiny to fulfill. Instead, it is a part of your individual journey back to your Divinity. Not only is this beneficially impacting your own human life, it is the evolutionary tract that is the solution for all of humanity's problems.

This leads to the third key in **Mastering Your Life,** which is to embrace Unity Consciousness. This involves taking our new understanding of our true higher identity, along with our present moment spiritual practice, and expressing and expanding this loving force out into the world. Unity Consciousness supports us in recognizing the Divinity in all humans, regardless of our perceived human differences.

In spite of the consistent "education" and indoctrination by our fear-based culture, we are all equal and worthy of the right to fulfill our unique life path on the highest level. Someone extremely enlightened once said, "Love thy neighbor as thy self." But unfortunately instead of that, we have created great separation, fear, and judgment of our fellow man.

Within our religions, governments, geographical boundaries, ideologies, races, etc. we have routinely condemned those outside of our own group, affiliation, or association. It is time for this to change, before it is too late. We must work to heal within and then recognize ourselves and all others with only love. It always starts with us first. Only you can heal you, just as only I can heal myself.

Within this higher space, we can express a whole new energy within every aspect of our lives. We can fulfill our higher purpose, which leads us to offer our greatest gifts in service to others. If enough people were to live an enlightened path, together we could solve all of the world's problems. Don't wait for "the other guy" to awaken, be the light of truth for others. Be an Enlightened Master.

Meditation Practice – a tool for Enlightened Living

A regular meditation practice is a powerful tool for claiming your present moment power and awakening to your Authentic Self. Something important to be aware of is that meditation is less about doing and more about being, which makes it a somewhat unique practice to modern day humans.

11

Its discipline asks not for exertion or assertion, and instead for allowing and accepting. We are required to let go and release the typically frantic energy that finds us in pursuit of some outward goal or random busyness. This instantly makes this challenging for most people, especially those of us raised in the U.S.

A regular meditation practice requires patient, consistent engagement within your own quiet inner space. This is a practice which reinforces that our life is always in process, and that we are more than our thoughts or activities. Our goal in this practice is to connect to the energy of our higher truth; hence this is a process of awakening. We focus on our breath, the one physical act that may only take place in the present moment.

Meditation has been an established practice for supporting healing and enlightenment for thousands of years. And while a key tool for enlightened living, it has never been especially easy for mankind. Now, as in ancient times, our mind tries to resist surrendering to the quiet power of our higher Self, or to reside in the present moment.

The act of maintaining this practice requires the more subtle, yet powerful, qualities of discipline, self-love, detachment, acceptance, and surrender. Again, these are all worthy qualities to help awaken and shift us to live all of our human experiences within a higher perspective. We now may begin to recognize and express our greater loving presence in all that we do.

Embarking on a meditation practice helps to solve many of the challenges we create for ourselves. Finding the space of self-realization in your meditation is creating time for "being." This not only relates to connecting with your Authentic Self, but also it is space for releasing the burden of disempowering thoughts, actions, interactions, and human distractions. For you this might lead to more moments throughout your hectic day to be reminded of this space that is always available with our awareness. And this may provide added clarity and peace, and will likely improve your expressions of energy and personal relationships. Additionally, it has been scientifically proven to be a great tool to combat stress, and its associated illnesses.

I strongly encourage you to establish your own regular meditation practice. In my *"Mastering Your Life"* book I have gone into some detail about how to begin, for those who are new to this discipline. You may use the information and methods that I have described there, or otherwise study techniques on your own. The greatest point is to just begin to get comfortable within this space of silence, and find your path to connecting to your Authentic Self for inner guidance and wellness. Just as in any spiritual practice, there is no one way to do this. So find the best path that honors you.

14

PART I:

REALIZING A HIGHER TRUTH

"I don't think that anything happens by coincidence ... no one is here by accident ... everyone who crosses our path has a message for us. Otherwise, they would have taken another path, left earlier or later. The fact that these people are here means that they are here for some reason."

- James Redfield

PART I: Prologue

The true higher value of our relationships is to support our own spiritual healing, growth, and evolution. Our relationships offer a primary tool for such a purpose. It then becomes essential for us to shift our awareness in realization of this truth, and discover the great potential for empowerment within our connection to other humans.

We have historically treated our relationships as if they are designed to make us feel better about ourselves, or otherwise give us what we think we need from others. The truth is that they are primarily designed to guide and teach us to recognize our own capability in meeting our own unique needs. We are given the opportunity to honor and facilitate our own inner wellness, as we find joy, fulfillment, and meaning on our journey. As we understand the higher truth of all beings, relationships are to be mutually beneficial and supportive to all.

To the extent to which we are unable to realize our higher path and purpose, our relationships become a tool to reflect back to us our need for more accountability and self-love. As we are able to recognize and learn our lessons, we may experience the healing, growth, and wellness that were the purpose of the relationship. When we ignore or misunderstand the true value of the experience, we will continue the unconsciousness that leads to more suffering – and more lessons.

PART I: Energetic Quality or Tool

The energetic quality I find most valuable for realizing a higher truth about relationships is **WISDOM**. This represents a higher form of knowledge, which is essential for an enlightened perspective. From this higher space of awareness we may elevate our understanding of all aspects of our human experience – including relationships.

The opposite quality is *IGNORANCE*. Often this is misunderstood as a judgment about one's intelligence or ability to think or reason. However, I consider this word to represent a barrier that limits or restricts awareness of the full view of our own higher truth. Even while highly intellectual, we may be stubborn or closed minded on matters of higher wisdom.

Wisdom utilizes both cognitive skills as well as the receptivity of a path of knowledge that may be beyond our physical senses. Nonetheless, this understanding is quite valuable and beneficial to our holistic wellness. We must be able to expand our field of awareness by connecting with our source of energy and truth within.

When doing so, within the topic of relationships, we will notice that a higher value exists, beyond our perceived human needs and desires. Therefore, relationships fulfill both a spiritual and human purpose for all people. As we are able to honor our unique gifts and life path, we may utilize the tool of relationships to support our healing, growth, and evolution. And we will likely be better positioned to love and honor all others as well. In this way we are integrating our Divinity into our humanity. This is Enlightened Wisdom.

CHAPTER 1
The Human Soul on Earth

"The soul is your innermost being. The presence that you are beyond form. The consciousness that you are beyond form, that is the soul. That is who you are in essence."

- Eckhart Tolle

In the highest spiritual realms of consciousness exists Oneness. Yet, simultaneously, each of us exists as a Soul, an individuation of the one Universal Consciousness or Divine Energy that permeates all things. Our Soul is on a journey to expand and evolve in some manner, and this has led us to Earth. You may call it Earth school, since this experience somehow develops us for the next phase of our existence. In any case, while we are here, it offers the potential for healing, growth, evolution, and service.

The unique path of our Soul is now involved in a unique human journey. From our own perspective and purpose, each person shares the goal of elevating their consciousness and integrating their spiritual nature into their human condition. With our Soul's designs for all of our specific qualities, gifts, and circumstances of this life, we start on our human path. This is intended to be an "Enlightened Path."

We are all here to experience our path to healing and expansion with and amongst other Souls who are on a similar journey. Presently, Earth holds approximately 7.2 billion humans/Souls. We are all working through the ego delusion that we have learned and attached to since birth. This effectively blocks or diminishes the awareness of our higher truth and identity. Somehow the advancement of our Soul, within the context of free will, requires this temporary diversion from our direct experience of unlimited access to Spirit. We have shifted into a much denser form of energy that holds us to our human physical nature.

So as part of our journey toward healing, growth, evolution, and service we are meant to transcend our human challenges. This is a transformation that will necessitate we learn a higher wisdom that rises above our false ego education. In some form or fashion this requires us to direct our free will toward an awakening (re-connecting) to our higher identity, and the elevation of our consciousness.

By shifting away from our lower ego-based energetic expressions and perceptions, we elevate to the higher expressions of loving energy, which is our true nature. As we continue to realize this truth, we will more often live in the power of our Divinity within all aspects of our humanity. We may call this our ongoing "spiritual" practice, because it exists within a higher intention than our normal ego desires. Yet, this is really our deciding to live the more enlightened path which our Soul intended.

The results of our efforts toward this transformation lead to our enlightenment as humans. But most importantly it supports our Soul's purposes. As we elevate our consciousness we accelerate our energetic vibration. This has the effect of expressing our light and loving presence into this human world, which elevates the collective consciousness.

A consequence of this is to fully recognize and honor all other human Souls, who are on their own journey of awakening. We thereby more easily offer our love and support to others. We can do this directly as we interact with the people in our lives. And we also may offer our light indirectly, both through our energy, and our example as enlightened humans, which others may emulate.

It is not merely a coincidence (or nuisance) that we are all here at this time. In some form or other, this is serving our higher purposes, both individually and collectively. So our most empowered view of life is to begin to accept that we are to work with each other for the benefit and ascension of all. This requires us to focus on healing ourselves and our relationships.

Obviously, while we are all here together on the planet, it is not practical for us to directly associate with everyone. So as part of our spiritual plan for this life, we have "contracted" with certain specific individual Souls. It is these connections that offer the experiences which become our primary lessons for healing, growth, and evolution. This is called a Soul Group. It consists of those closest to us, family, friends, and even those whom we may have falsely labeled our enemies. In addition to the value of these lessons in our life, there is also a matter of karmic balancing with these other Souls. This simply means that we have experienced a previous life path together where we left some unfinished energetic business that needs to be resolved or released.

As you observe the current state of human relations you may consider our healing to be a matter of some urgency. We are designed to work together, to be supportive and share our many gifts and higher loving qualities. Yet our history shows something very different. Our lower energetic ego-nature has ruled humanity to this point. Our relationships, whether as close to us as our birth family, or as seemingly separate from us as our scattered human family, must be considered important and valuable.

An enlightened view of relationships is much more than dealing with your partner or dating, your friends or co-workers, or someone that hassles you. It is really reflective of the quality of your own inner consciousness, relating to all other human Souls. Certainly our time and daily focus is more connected with certain specific people in our lives. And this will be the majority focus in this book. However, we also have a responsibility to observe higher expressions of love for all people. We have the privilege of encouraging and honoring everyone else who is on their human path and spiritual journey.

Even if all we can do for others is refraining from judgement and condemnation of them, this is higher service.

All of this may extend beyond what you normally think about "relationships." There certainly exists the day to day human involvement that we all experience. However, there are reasons and purposes for all that exists when you are willing to expand to a higher truth. And your accountability for your thoughts, words, and actions greatly influences the quality of life for all. This is the primary wisdom teaching in this book. It is supportive toward achieving a higher perspective that leads to a life of greater understanding, fulfillment, appreciation, and potential for love and wellness.

CHAPTER 2
The First Truth about Relationships

"The only journey is the journey within."

- Rainer Maria Rilke

The first truth is that our relationships are spiritual tools within our human experience. They enable us to recognize our degree of alignment with our own higher identity – Divinity. This can also be expressed as our connection to our Authentic Self. Relationships offer the experiences and exchanges of energy that are meant to serve a purpose of inner healing and growth, leading to wellness and outer service.

They offer lessons that provide an opportunity for us to accumulate wisdom that is supportive to our evolution and success. But this is only available when we are willing and accountable for receiving this truth and then taking appropriate action. When we are unable to do this, the teaching does not go away, for we are always attracting what we need. In fact, the severity will likely escalate, in order to get your attention. You may have unwittingly "chosen" to sign-up for the more challenging follow-up lessons. Your Soul's purpose is to evolve, and since you were unable to do this through higher awareness, you are now required to learn through unconscious repetition until you do acquire what you need to advance.

In this matter, you were aligned with your ego and not Spirit. These experiences are actually blessings, though they may not feel that way at the time. This is simply your Spirit guiding you back to your higher truth. When you are

23

accountable and mindful regarding your relationship attractions and interactions, you will be choosing to learn in the present through empowerment. You may then move forward to the next level of interaction, growth, wellness, etc.

When we do not choose to be accountable for our energetic expressions and attractions, we will simply continue on our path in a state of relative darkness (ignorance). We will encounter various people to teach us when and how we are not honoring our purpose of healing and growth; when we are expressing fear (in some form) instead of love. Typically, these experiences are challenging to our humanity, and we may not "awaken" until we have experienced a measure of suffering. Yet these involvements are merely a reflection of the inner darkness that we have allowed to control and create our outer experience.

The quality of your inner wellness will then become your expressions of energy out into the world. From this space you will attract your relationships. People who are connected in a more loving and supportive way are primarily expressing loving energy to each other. This means that on some level their inner state is connected to love or higher truth, whether or not they would use this terminology.

However, even an individual in the loving relationship above may have other relationships, or even a general perception of some group of people, that is antagonistic and negative. This means that they are manifesting certain unhealthy relationships as a result of some inner energetic quality based in fear. This energy is the delusion of the lower ego-self being transmitted into the world. While on a path of enlightened awareness, you will realize this when observing the negative tenor of these relationships.

When conscious you will be accountable for your own energetic expressions. Therefore, when someone is expressing fearful or negative thoughts toward or about you, you have a choice to make. Am I going to accept their expressions and shift my energy into defending myself and retaliating (which is fear)?

Or am I going to take this opportunity to hold my own loving space, and then, more objectively, consider any potential lesson? Maybe they are my teacher and not a perpetrator. In any case, we learn when we can, and we are working to release judgment and fear.

Only you can choose to heal you. Fighting with others serves no real purpose toward elevating your wellness. While your ego may feel a bit bruised in the process, a valuable purpose will be served by taking this higher perspective. If another person seems unsupportive or judgmental with their words, check your own thoughts and feelings. It is likely that you have attracted this outer energy by harboring some fear, doubt, or insecurity within yourself first.

Your fighting against them is a form of agreeing with them. It is a confirmation of your inner negative self-belief. Otherwise, remain in your loving truth, and decide not to attach to their expressions, which in reality only define **their** view and beliefs. Make the intentional effort to shift your inner dialogue to something that better supports your self-love and higher truth. And then reflect only loving expressions to others.

While endeavoring to live on the enlightened path we may notice the opportunities for growth in all relationships. We are living within an elevated state of awareness, and our intentions toward inner wellness are strong. Yet, transformation is not easy, the force of positive energy required to transcend our ego and shift to higher consciousness can be like leaving gravity – very challenging to our humanity.

We are facing our fear and vulnerability in order to stretch ourselves and honor our true path and purpose, which is quite contrary to our education. While our intentions are strong, we may still have great self-doubt and a preponderance of the old self-limiting beliefs. Naturally, this energy is expressed to some degree out into our world, thereby attracting someone to come along and doubt or challenge us.

Again, this is where our inner development is critical and most prized. Within a challenging situation, we are being shown that a degree of disconnection from our Authentic Self exists. But now, with wisdom, we have a chance to recover (quiet our ego) within a few breaths, and re-align with Spirit. We now may facilitate further healing by choosing love, which reinforces our inner power and enthusiasm.

The degree to which we are out of alignment, determines the impact of the negative expressions upon us. If we have worked sufficiently through some aspect of life, and in this respect our inner fear is very slight, our reaction to the comments of another will be slight as well. Have you ever had someone make a derogatory statement to you that was so far out of your self-belief system that you simply dismissed it outright? This is because your energy found no real basis to attach validity to their expressions. *The great lesson here is that any words spoken to or about you by another person have no true value other than that which you are willing to give them.*

However, if a person says something negative to you that directly connects with some deeply held negative self-belief, you have a whole different matter on your hands. This one may hurt a bit, because your ego delusion is heavily invested in this false belief. The lesson is the same, in that you attracted someone to show you where you are in need of healing in order to facilitate your inner wellness.

Your actual truth is that, while not perfect in your humanity, you are perfect in your Divinity, and doing the best you can on your unique life path. Therefore, the "damaging" inner belief and their external expression is not your truth. Awakening to this wisdom supports your process of healing and growth, and you will continue to encounter these "teachers" in your life until you are able to fully realize your own higher truth.

Of course, not all relationships are filled with challenging lessons, only the ones where we are encased in fear – controlled by ego. As you are able to express more from your inner connection to love, you will attract more loving, supportive relationships. Yet, even within our most positive,

26

enjoyable relationships we will still encounter lessons for the sake of our growth and ascension.

These lessons may serve to lead us to inner healing, yet they are expressed and received in a much more gentle and supportive tone. We have grown to love and trust our self enough to attract another person in whom we recognize love and trust. The more we can do this within, the more we will manifest this without. This is the purpose of teaching a higher truth. It supports a higher quality of life.

Certainly we will have some relationships where we share a positive and supportive energy, for the primary purpose of achievement, enjoyment, or service. As always, we are expressing our inner energy out into the world, and attracting another to participate in our experience. This may be a brief encounter or a life-long relationship. We create these experiences throughout our life for our own purposes. Yet they all will impact our humanity according to our energetic condition at the time.

You chose these human Souls as "partners" in your evolution. And this means that in some way you are to interact and learn some aspect of your truth that is supportive to the fulfillment of your purpose. This is true regardless of the human association, whether family, friend, co-worker, or other.

Once on the enlightened path, we may continue to elevate our consciousness and go beyond the task of seeking only positive, joyful relationships that support our comfort. There are higher levels to which we may ascend. We might be guided to find a meaningful purpose in sharing our light with all, whether or not they are supportive in return. There is an aspect of unconditional love that is possible to attain through self-mastery and alignment with Spirit.

CHAPTER 3
Energetic Attraction

"That which is like unto itself is drawn."

- Jerry and Esther Hicks

Our essence is Spirit, even while in human form. We and all things are simply energy. Within our relationships we express and attract energy with another person. In other words, the quality of our energy vibrates at a similar frequency, and when combined may facilitate the resolution of some higher purpose. This frequency is aligned with our inner energetic state.

We have access to the higher energetic qualities of Divinity, such as love, peace, joy, gratitude, compassion, unity, etc. These are said to vibrate at a faster rate. Accordingly, the Divine Beings, like Spirit Guides and Angels, are consistently vibrating at a level higher than humans. This makes direct contact difficult for most people, but does not diminish their existence, or benefit to us.

As humans, while we may access the higher Divine qualities, we most often have labored in the lower frequencies of ego. When we are more conscious and connected to our true identity our energy frequency will be higher, faster, and lighter. We are *en-LIGHT-ened*. Yet, while controlled by ego and the lower qualities of fear – such as, anger, judgment, hate, greed, resentment, insecurity, lack, etc. – we are said to vibrate lower, slower, and heavier. I am sure that you can sense this in your own experience.

Based upon the predominant quality of our energy, we create all manner of experiences and relationships that are compatible with our inner energetic state. Since our experiences are typically connected to other people, we share some compatible energy expression with them. The combination of these expressions will likely dictate the human quality, and reveal the true purpose of the relationship.

What we express eventually manifests into what we attract. This is a spiritual law. And it is evidence of the creative force that comes from our higher identity. When we are connected to our own Divinity, we abide in Love. And as we are able to express this quality it will be reflected in relationships and experiences that offer more love back to us.

However, when we become unconscious (disconnected from Spirit) we typically fall under the delusions of ego and we express our lower base energy of fear. As we are living from this space we attract this compatible form of energy with people who match this lower vibration. Thus they will reflect to us the lower qualities that we ourselves are in need of healing. We may not be aware of these inner negative qualities, yet if we attracted this person, we can be assured that they are there.

We often misunderstand the truth of a relationship as we are judging the quality of various positive and negative outcomes or experiences. We recognize that within a relationship there is some good and some (maybe mostly) bad – but I just need to see them differently, try harder, be patient, etc. We may want to think that the problem is our inability to love them unconditionally. Yet in truth, most of our thoughts express our desire for THEM to love us unconditionally. Both of these views are delusion.

The truth is that they are a mirror of you! You attracted them to reflect your need to offer unconditional love to you. It is always about you, on the level of energy. And if it isn't, then you do not understand your higher truth and purpose for being here. If you more often honored your truth and were accountable for your self-love and wellness, you would not need to experience a harmful or disempowering relationship. Therefore, you would have no cause to attract one.

From our ego perspective we are happy to notice that we attract more loving and peaceful encounters when we are satisfied with ourselves. This may have come from our own intentional focus on personal healing and growth. Or it may just be one of those natural fluctuations of our energy that ebbs and flows to some degree. We like to take credit, or otherwise appreciate, when things are going well.

As an aside, I always marvel when I hear someone say, "God is good," within only pleasant or positive circumstances. The inference being, where is God when "bad" things happen? My awareness tells me that the energy of God or the Divine is only love (or good), how we choose to perceive that which occurs around us is an indication of our connection to the Divine, and not a reflection upon it.

However, our lessons come in all kinds of energetic packages. And our greatest lessons – that indicate the need for major healing – seem to come from experiences that are most distressful to our humanity. We have missed the gentler clues that previous relationships endeavored to teach us. Now we are forced to face our truth and look within for the answers to our healing, growth, and evolution. Healing is always an inside job.

Our need for this level of awakening typically comes from a relationship that manifests as great suffering. We may have attracted a "teacher" that seems to have very little regard for our wellness, security, or happiness. This makes sense. They are reflecting back to us the extent to which we have abandoned our Authentic Self, and our responsibility for facilitating our own wellness, security, and happiness.

We may blame them as the cause for our troubles. And it is true that on a human level this person may be detestable in their behavior. However, the higher truth remains that we have allowed or supported this relationship due to our own unconscious behavior and refusal to be fully accountable for ourselves. Thus, our energy attracted someone to show us from the outside what we are doing to ourselves within.

By the way, we are a teacher to them as well, for they attracted us. So whether or not you think you signed up for that job, spiritual law dictates that you did. How they choose to deal with their needs for inner healing is up to them, and not you. Simply do your best to honor yourself, and release them with love.

All of spiritual awareness and development deals with managing our expressions of energy, and redirecting them to love. And all of this supports our well-being as humans. So we are best supported by understanding the higher value of our relationships. There is no opportunity for accountability when we believe that random bad things and bad people just show up in our life. This is how a victim lives their life. And you are not a victim.

Life and energy does not work that way. There is nothing random about Divine truth, even if we cannot always explain or understand it at the time. With higher awareness there is a great spiritual value and purpose to all of your relationships. You are each drawn together by a compatible energetic vibration, and this serves your purpose for healing, growth, evolution, and service.

Everything in existence potentially serves a higher purpose. Seek to understand and accept the value of each of your relationships as a higher path of wisdom. On this level, offer love and appreciation to all teachers. But most of all, connect with the loving energy that is your true identity, in order to shift to a more loving, joyful, and empowering experience within your relationships.

CHAPTER 4
Fulfilling a Human Purpose

"Destiny is not a matter of chance, it is a matter of choice. It is not a thing to be waited for, it is a thing to be achieved."

- William Jennings Bryan

Certainly we have been educated to think of relationships as fulfilling a human purpose. It is quite natural for us to more easily understand and accept this concept. In order to sustain our lifestyle, we need to work with other people (co-workers, bosses, customers, and other associates) on a regular basis. In order to fulfill our desire for companionship we have connections with friends and partners for a more intimate personal sharing of experiences. Then, for whatever role we play in our family, such as child, parent, grandparent, or other, we may express a deep caring as we seek to utilize each other's support.

All of these relationships arise with the intent of a mutual sharing of energy leading to some human achievement or level of satisfaction. We essentially believe that this other person will support us in filling some need. Hopefully, there is also an effort on our part to support them as well. Even if this is not equal in every instance, on the balance, it should even out over time. Healthy relationships involve give and take, and at least the intention to be mutually beneficial.

Our first thought, from the perspective of ego might be, "I believe that I need _____, therefore, I will engage this person in some form of relationship." Especially early in life; when our primary point of view is based upon getting our needs met by others. Depending upon our upbringing, and the extent to which we can develop maturity, we will shift toward more consideration about the other involved. Yet this inner development varies from person to person, and for some this rarely seems to happen.

Two issues standout for me. One, we have been conditioned to rely upon others when it may be most supportive for us to do for ourselves. And two, when we consciously decide that something would be more satisfying, rewarding, or successful in partnership with another person, we must be able to value and honor their needs as well as ours.

So the concept of transcending relationships works on both the spiritual and human levels. There is a need within each of us to develop our inner wellness through the healing and maintenance of our energy. And this inner work will always serve a useful purpose in cultivating fulfilling and rewarding human relations.

Regarding our taking responsibility for our own wellness, healing, growth, and ascension, this we must ultimately do for ourselves. We can learn a higher education, be inspired, and observe enlightened role models, but in the end we must be fully accountable for our own energy. And as we now know, it is our expressions of energy that truly create our external experiences.

Any significant deficit in our own energy will be a detriment to the quality our many relationships and interactions. We connect with a partner, with the intention of sharing our lives, yet we enter this arrangement filled with false self-beliefs and fear-based energy. Therefore, our best intentions will not create the results we desire. Eventually we will expect the other person to offer the level of love and consideration that only we can give to ourselves. And if this is your energy, there is a good chance that they have unrealistic expectations of you as well. It is only a matter of time before this inner conflict manifests into outer behavior that brings mistrust, hurt feelings, and the potential for extreme dissatisfaction.

Certainly, it is an option to learn your lessons about being accountable for your inner needs within a relationship structure. While living unconscious we all will learn this way. Just know that this is not ideal from the standpoint of your human satisfaction. You may think that you are getting your needs met through this person. Maybe you want intimacy, companionship, financial support, shared outer responsibilities, etc. Yet, depending upon the type of commitment involved, you are agreeing to accept their expectations of you as well. And as you now must share your time and energy within additional activities and associations, this may be more than you bargained for.

Therefore, in addition to your own accountability for inner wellness, you must be fully cognizant of the totality of the relationship's expectations and duties. You may or may not have believed that you are completely capable of meeting your own needs alone. Regardless, you have chosen a relationship, so now you must expand your energy and awareness. Initially you will want to explore and consider all of the key issues for each of you. Evaluate and communicate honestly. There will likely need to be some compromise, which is fine so long as you are not required to dishonor yourself or abandon your truth. Always honor your own truth. In the end this will greatly serve your partner as well.

You will need to develop and practice a greater awareness of your impact on others and their impact upon you. You are sharing energetic space. How you think, feel, speak, and act toward or around each other matters. You won't be perfect, but with a heightened level of awareness you will avoid many unnecessary conflicts and negativity. When you have fallen into an ego trap, regain your truth and take corrective action as quickly as possible. Now you may support each other and build upon a strong foundation of loving energy.

Obviously this is most pertinent to spouses or intimate partner relationships, but it is also true for all other potentially-empowering relationships. Be accountable for your own wellness.

Honestly communicate your needs and expectations. Be prepared to honor their needs and expectations. Compromise where appropriate. Elevate your awareness of the impact of your energetic expressions toward each other.

We have a human purpose to share love and friendship, support and service. We are here to help each other. So why do we see so much fear, fighting, mistrust, judgment, and anger? Why are so many people unable or barely able to meet their human needs for survival? And why are so many others stuck in lives filled with dissatisfaction and lack of purpose or passion?

We have chosen to spend this time (however long it will be) as part of our Soul's journey in human form. And many of us are not living up to the potential we all possess. We know that this time won't last forever, so we get selfish, stingy, and uncompassionate toward others. Our goal has been to focus on our own physical desires, and maybe those of our close family, to the exclusion of all others.

We have falsely judged our human purpose as the pursuit of power and avoidance of lack. Some will think or say, "The extent of my wealth and extravagance is my business. Even if you are starving and homeless, that's your problem, not mine." Yet, this attitude of division and selfishness is not fulfilling to our Spirit, nor is it serving our humanity. No one is going to take their wealth with them after they die, and in the meantime, people are suffering and dying needlessly. The point is for each of us to consider a more enlightened, balanced, and compassionate approach to our life and humanity.

Fulfilling a human purpose goes beyond the state of your own physical well-being. Accountability for your inner wellness is the key to supporting you and all others on the level of Unity Consciousness. We may develop inner love, peace, joy, abundance, gratitude, compassion, and reverence. Now we can express these qualities out into the world for the benefit of all. More people who need help will get help, from more people willing and able to give it.

Sure, we must prioritize our physical needs as a way of continuing this journey. Yet, there are levels to which we become unhealthy, unbalanced, and unsupportive. Express the quality of love in all of your relationships and you will find greater personal satisfaction within all of your experiences, while being supportive to others. Make the highest purpose of your work to offer value and service into the world, and not just the accumulation of wealth and possessions. Oh, by the way, you will receive greater personal fulfillment, often leading to a higher quality of life.

This way of fulfilling a human purpose on the enlightened path is available to each of us. Simply open your heart and mind to realize a higher truth. Greater inner strength leads to sufficiency and gratitude, which leads to greater love and service to others. Be empowered to help more people be empowered.

CHAPTER 5
Know Thy Self

"You have to grow from the inside out. None can teach you, none can make you spiritual. There is no other teacher but your own soul."

- Swami Vivekananda

The best path for honoring your truth in the fulfillment of your humanity is to endeavor to accept and understand your unique life. And then persevere within the application and development of your specific gifts, talents, purpose, and passion. As you focus on your strengths you will learn to realize your value and understand your purpose. This is a shift in energy and self-image that will greatly support you in this life.

When we have done a sufficient amount of inner healing work we can have a greater appreciation and acceptance of who we are, and what we came here to do. Therefore, endeavor to know thy self. We must know and honor our truth before we may begin to create relationships that honor our truth. Yet, how is this possible if we do not really know our own power and value?

What is most important to you in a relationship or career? What qualities in another are most supportive to your wellness? What are you most passionate about? What are you good at, and want to develop further? What are the other qualities that you want to improve on? What is it that you most want to experience? Take the time and make the effort to examine your life. It was Plato who said, "The life unexamined is not worth living." This is the only life you have, so make it count. This is an important part of being accountable. There is no wellness or enlightenment without accountability.

Know yourself first. How can you really expect satisfying long-term relationships without knowing yourself? How will you know what to look or ask for from another person? How can you truly support them until you know who you are?

Then continue to learn and examine your life. If you are living well you are healing, growing, and evolving. So your potential should be ascending. Honor and cultivate this higher path.

As you begin to know yourself you will create the circumstances and conditions that are most supportive of your specific brand of wellness, success, and satisfaction. Knowing yourself implies your TRUE self. Therefore, you first must begin to unlearn the false perceptions that you were previously taught about yourself. We have developed an entire identity out of what others want us to be or do with our life. This is very disempowering. And the longer we delay in claiming our truth, the harder it becomes to transcend the delusion. Ultimately this may require a shift on the level of awakening, which then redirects you to your best path.

Do the inner work toward identifying your Authentic Self. Through this work, as well as taking an objective view of your experiences, you will uncover your truth. Your Spirit has always known your truth. This is why we must connect to this higher part of ourselves.

Now, the real moment to moment work of honoring your Authentic Self begins. Within your relationships you will be given many opportunities to fall back into the old false, fear-based persona. Others have defined you according to their own perceptions and beliefs. While pursuing your truth, do not be detoured or limited by the many "well-intentioned" people giving their advice or criticism. Will you choose to honor the real you? Or will you revert back to the false you in order to please others? In this you will learn the meaning of courage, and begin to walk your own enlightened path.

This is part of the purpose of relationship. These people are not there to harass you; they are reflecting the energy of doubt that still remains within you. Therefore, be kind, but always trust yourself. Heed only the advice or feedback that is supportive for your higher purposes. Learn to listen to your intuition and not your ego. One promotes love and advancement, while the other fear and restriction.

In considering the creation of new relationships, be mindful of expressing your truth. As you begin to live more enlightened this becomes easier, because those you meet now are judging the present you, instead of the past disempowered you. Spend less time convincing the people you knew before, and more time expanding your light and truth toward new relationships. You will find this empowering.

Don't simply look for someone to mask your "weaknesses." Work to become a whole person. This is the integration of your spirituality within your humanity. The "you complete me" fallacy that the world has sold you is a license to be unaccountable for your own wellness, and insecure in your own power. You cannot be fulfilled as a spiritual/human being this way. Remember, you are the Master of your life.

Instead, look to offer your best qualities in your relationships. Appreciate their best qualities as they are offered back to you. We each have different gifts, skills, passion, and talents to offer the world. This is why they are called unique. Certainly you will match your energy and truth with that of the other person.

You are essentially shifting from the mindset that it is all about having your needs met by the other, to each person being accountable and empowered. When you are each offering your best loving energy and living your true identity, you will create the healthiest and most supportive conditions. You will find greater satisfaction, fulfillment, and appreciation for each other. And ascension will be inevitable.

41

CHAPTER 6

Release the Victim Identity

"Death is not the biggest fear we have; our biggest fear is taking the risk to be alive – the risk to be alive and express what we really are."

- Don Miguel Ruiz

You are never to identify yourself as a victim. You are more powerful than your experiences. While you may have temporarily created or attracted circumstances or conditions that are highly unsupportive to your well-being, your purpose is to take the steps to reclaim your power and redirect your path. Align with your higher truth and endeavor to know yourself for your value and strengths, and not for your wounds.

This is primarily an inner focus that supports you toward living in the present and releasing the past. Yet, it also may entail a change in scenery and certain relationships. You want to be fully accountable for shifting within and without in ways that honor your healing, growth, and ascension to higher consciousness. The true purpose of your experience was to teach you, not punish you. And it was not arbitrary or just bad luck. So get about the business of learning and moving forward as quickly and earnestly as possible.

This is not to be taken as unsympathetic or uncaring. In truth, recognizing ourselves and others as powerful beings and not powerless victims is the highest form of caring and compassion. Many human experiences can be quite painful and distressing, and I am not saying that transcending them is easy or quick. However, it is the only path that supports your wellness.

Everyone has experienced something or many things that were hurtful or devastating on some level. Of course, we have attracted this energy in order to support our deeper healing and redirect us in some way. However, when we are unwilling to do this, we will create the suffering that turns into a victim mentality. This then becomes a significant part of our false identity. It is completely disempowering. When in this lower energetic state we may be so distraught that normal day-to-day functions become difficult. Or, we may exist by pulling the energy of others through sympathy and martyrdom.

In fact, we must be very careful in how we identify with our challenges. Beyond the propensity to stay stuck in victim mentality, I notice that even when we overcome our challenge we may retain our identity as a "survivor." Whether the condition is physical or psychological, transcending means releasing our previous limitations, and claiming a new higher position. Our goal is to live well in the present, which leads to our greatest opportunities in the future. We can certainly find great purpose in supporting those bearing a situation in which we were previously afflicting. However, learn to live from your higher identity, in support of theirs.

Any victim-laden persona becomes a destructive place from which to create a relationship. This is likely to be highly co-dependent, and promote great negativity and dissatisfaction. It is looking for external solutions (other people) to fix an internal problem. This is because your energy is controlled by fear. In order to discontinue repeating your disempowering experiences, you need to be more accountable to yourself and reclaim your true identity that is based in the energy of love.

As a part of the inner healing, you must accept on a deep level that the experience in question was supportive to all involved on a higher level. Maybe someone close to you passes away, or a relationship ends, or some other significant human hardship befalls you. From the point of view of the victim, we often do not want to believe that this was in any way beneficial.

We are entirely focused upon how we are personally negatively impacted within our humanity. This is the perspective of ego.

Sometimes the things that happen in our lives are only peripherally connected to us, and primarily for someone else involved. Yet, when we make everything about us, we create our own suffering. This is the interesting thing about relationships. We are always walking the line of personal accountability and higher identity, and attachment to other people and the corresponding human identity.

If someone's Earthly journey ends who is close to us, we will experience many challenging thoughts and emotions. We understand that our life will no longer be the same. However, when our identity is so connected (attached) to this other person, as to obscure our own truth, we will suffer, even though the triggering event was primarily for the person who died. Obviously this is a natural process. Yet, it is for us to come to the most empowered understanding and healing, in order to transcend and shift our energy. On another level, all relationship endings bring this need for inner healing.

It is only our unwillingness to be accountable for re-connected to our own higher power and identity that leaves us continually stuck in victim mode. There is not a person who will ever walk this Earth who will not have this experience. It is for us to be supportive and compassionate for others in need. However, only we can heal ourselves. Only we can choose to see a higher path and purpose that goes beyond this world. And only the Universal Divinity knows how each of these events is entirely supportive to our highest evolution and purpose.

Regarding the ultimate benefit to us on our Soul journey, we must rely on Faith. However, as an approach to enlightened living, we can know that choosing to accept the higher value in all of our experiences will offer the greatest support to our humanity. Transcending relationships pertains to all phases of each of our interpersonal connections, and how to best navigate our own truth and wellness within these experiences.

CHAPTER 7
Introvert or Extrovert

"To be yourself in a world that is constantly trying to make you something else is the greatest accomplishment."

- Ralph Waldo Emerson

As we begin to more deeply honor our unique gifts, qualities, passions, and purpose, we will become more aware of our natural form of energetic expression, relative to how we interact with others. Our ultimate goal is to live our humanity while in alignment with our truth. As we understand ourselves better we may learn to live more in our own flow and rhythm, and accept that this is right for us.

How we express our energy and fortify our inner power is important to understand. Not all people are the same. The common terms introvert and extrovert refer to the nature of your outer expressions that support your inner value for wellness and empowerment. It is also a feature of the personality that you chose. Neither is better or worse, so simply honor and utilize whichever classification you believe serves you best.

As an extrovert you will likely be more inclined to vocalize and otherwise express your energy in outer communications and even bodily/facial expressions. You may be more comfortable in the spotlight, initiating conversations, or being in large crowds. As you interact with others in a more demonstrative way, you feel energized and empowered. You may be more outwardly assertive. Your emphasis may be more about DOING (controlling). This reflects a part of your higher truth. Accepting this quality may lead you into relationships, experiences, and careers that best utilize your gifts. Particularly any profession that regularly deals with other people, such as: sales, customer service, promotion, public speaking, teaching, law, politics, and many more.

Being an introvert supports a different way of expressing your energy. In this case, your greatest inner strength comes from relative solitude, or associations within smaller groups. You may be more thoughtful and contemplative before speaking. Your energy may be more scattered and displaced in crowds, which leaves you feeling less empowered. As opposed to seeking the spotlight, you may be more content behind the scenes, and in letting others initiate conversations. Your emphasis may be more on BEING (allowing). This reflects a part of your higher truth.

Your motivations are more inner driven and may support you in fulfilling your value in creative, meditative, and analytical endeavors. Honoring this quality may lead you to relationships, experiences, and careers that best utilize your gifts. You may feel most comfortable and successful in professions that are more autonomous, such as: writer, artist, accountant, researcher, scientist, engineer, and many more.

This is not a black or white analysis, nor meant to be restrictive, as we are relatively unlimited as to our potential for interaction and expression. However, we do have predominant qualities, and honoring our truth will empower us. So long as we are each honoring ourselves and the truth of others, relationships that encompass each quality can be most effective and rewarding.

Within the context of relationships, we often have a tendency to partner with a person on the opposite side of this coin. There is a combined balancing that may be satisfying to each of us. Yet, this is only true when we are honoring ourselves and each other. If not, we can easily be annoyed or disappointed in our partner due to their different way of processing and communicating. As an enlightened partner, learn what is most fulfilling, empowering, and rewarding for them. Then make a conscious choice to support them as often as possible in this way.

If your tendency is to naturally express your energy as an introvert, you may want to explore your opportunities to expand the breadth of your power externally. If you function more naturally as an extrovert, you might focus on expanding the depth of your power internally. For the sake of growth and healing we may occasionally choose to step outside of our comfort zone with awareness and intention, as we notice the occasion to create new opportunities or otherwise seek greater balance.

Build your power by focusing on your strengths and natural gifts. Do not feel that you must express or experience your life the way others do, in order to be valued. Knowing and honoring your truth will serve you best. You may notice that my natural energy tends toward being introverted. So my teaching in wisdom and wellness involves a primary focus on inner development. An extrovert writing a similar book may instead stress building relationships by networking or just getting out there in a bold way. There is no one way or one truth for everyone. Simply honor your best path.

PART I: Exercises

1) Take some time to document what you believe to be your true unique human gifts, skills, qualities, passions, and purpose. Are you an introvert or extrovert, and how might you utilize this as a strength? What other personality traits do you possess? As you look at the above, are you generally honoring your truth, or trying to be, or satisfy, someone else? Are you generally expressing your truth in your relationships?

2) In a quiet contemplative state, consider and document your current key relationships. List their primary role (ex. partner, friend, family member, co-worker, etc.). Now document the human needs that you are asking them to fulfill. Is this reasonable, healthy, and appropriate? Then consider how, beyond their human purpose, they may represent an opportunity to support your spiritual healing and growth?

3) How does your inner energetic knowing align with the external conditions of these relationships? Are you primarily expressing love or fear? Can you notice an opportunity to utilize this relationship to honor your truth and heal on a deeper level?

PART I: Affirmations

I AM now fulfilling a higher purpose in all of my relationships.

I AM now expressing only loving energy to all.

I AM now attracting only empowering relationships.

I AM now honoring myself in all of my relationships.

I AM now honoring my truth.

I AM empowered.

I AM loving and lovable.

I AM now living my life on purpose.

I AM fully accountable for loving myself.

I AM expressing my love and truth out into the world.

I AM always attracting loving relationships.

PART II:

LEARNING AND HEALING FROM THE PAST

"Because I trust in the ever-changing climate of the heart, I think it is necessary to have many experiences for the sake of feeling something; for the sake of being challenged, and for the sake of being expressive, to offer something to someone else, to learn what we are capable of."

- Jason Mraz

PART II: Prologue

This Section focuses on your past relationships. All of these have created countless experiences designed to teach you important lessons about your true value and potential. This is essential toward fulfilling the higher purpose of your unique life path. When we are conscious (connected to our higher truth in the present moment) we will reap the great benefits of these lessons that are leading us to more love, peace, and wellness. However, most of us have accumulated many disabling false perceptions and beliefs due to our unconsciousness within many of our past relationships.

It is this disempowering view of you that must be addressed and healed. It is likely that specific experiences or certain relationships in general have triggered many human challenges and much suffering. Yet, through accountability these are valuable opportunities to awaken and re-align your life. Therefore, begin to honor your truth and facilitate the healing that is needed now.

With a greater realization of the higher truth about our energetic attractions, we may shift into learning/healing mode, and away from victim mode. With higher wisdom we can rightfully offer forgiveness and appreciation for the past. Then we become more empowered and conscious as we heal, grow, and evolve in the present. From your earliest relationships of family to your most recent interpersonal connections, you have actually been supported on your path. Nothing is wasted – everything has been preparing you to choose your greatest empowerment now. Own this higher reality. It is time to claim your power, honor your truth, and to learn and apply the wisdom from past relationships.

PART II: Energetic Quality or Tool

Regarding the concept of learning and healing from the past, the energetic qualities that I have been given to share are **RELEASE** and **NON-ATTACHMENT**. As you examine your past relationships with a new higher perspective, you may apply the quality of Release as part of your healing process. Release the old disempowering energy, and utilize Non-attachment within your current relationships moving forward.

The opposite quality is called **ATTACHMENT**, and is typically the beginning of the end of the higher value to be shared in a relationship. This is because, through fear, we have attached our energy to another person or outer expectation. This ultimately cuts us off from our own power. We are effectively giving away our power, instead of living in the present and being accountable for our own energetic wellness.

While unconscious, disconnected from our higher identity and love, we were required to learn our lessons through suffering (in some form). As we engaged in this past relationship we each expressed and retained negative energy. This, therefore, requires our inner healing by reclaiming our own loving energy, and the releasing of any negative energy we may be holding from the other person.

Having learned the consequences of attachment, we now endeavor to maintain our own highest energy while interacting and associating with others. In addition to our regular practice of mindfulness, we do this by utilizing the quality of Non-Attachment. As we participate in our relationships we must focus our awareness on our own inner energetic state. This also requires us to allow others to live in their space. When honoring our truth, we should be able to realize our level of energetic wellness without the necessity of outer suffering.

CHAPTER 8

You Must Be Fully Accountable

"Your task is not to seek love, but merely to seek and find all of the barriers within yourself that you have built against it."

- Rumi

As you move through the chapters in Part II, the main goal and focus will always be for you to take full accountability for yourself. This includes all of your experiences and relationships. This is your life, and your opportunity to facilitate your own healing, growth, and evolution. If I believed that other people were accountable for creating your path and reality, then there would be no point in teaching this wisdom. When you accept your true power to create your life for the better, you will rightfully understand that your expressions of energy do, indeed, matter. This ultimately creates your best life and wellness.

There is one point that I want to be clear about in the beginning. While you have energetically attracted your relationships which have led to your experiences, you are not responsible for the actions of others. They have attracted you in support of their own process of healing and growth. They are responsible for themselves, while you are responsible for you. In this way you may accept the "teacher" and the lesson, without condoning or accepting accountability for the unloving thoughts, words, and actions of other people.

On this human path we are striving to heal, grow, and evolve in a way that supports our awakening to enlightened living. This entails the shifting and transcending of our previous perception of a limited reality. Our reality will always be limited when we attempt to control others or define our joy and success based upon what others do. In fact, any expectations that we have, regarding other people solving our problems, will likely lead to dissatisfaction. This is because facilitating our wellness is our job and not theirs. It is for us to elevate our awareness and identity in order to experience our Divine qualities within our humanity. And all of your relationship experiences have been trying to teach you this truth all along.

The aim of the wisdom taught in this book is to guide you toward creating and experiencing more transcendent relationships. In this way you will find greater fulfillment in connection with other human Souls, both in support of your mutual wellness and service. All of your past relationships have reflected your views and beliefs about yourself and the world around you. Now, with an understanding of your potential for greater self-love and empowerment, you are able to examine your past relationships using higher awareness.

This is not an exercise in reliving the energetic deficits that have brought so much suffering through misunderstanding and fear. Instead, it is an opportunity for you to understand your role and purpose in these relationships as they relate to healing and growth. This examination must be made through full accountability. Yet, it is from your perspective about yourself, and need not be approved or verified by anyone else.

You will endeavor to release any attachments to other people, and to the disempowering beliefs about yourself. Within this present space, connected to your true identity, you have the power and the freedom to be more objective regarding the emotional impact of certain challenging past experiences. This is a higher point of observation (a spiritual view), understanding that even when we experience great ego pain, our Spirit is never harmed. You are looking to recognize your role and energetic needs, in order to gain self-awareness, understanding, and wisdom.

My hope is that by the end of Part II you will have a better understanding of the purpose and benefit of the lessons from your past relationships. Yes, even the ones that brought unfathomable suffering. You must elevate from the lower energy of ego and take a higher view. The ego wants to blame others, which is evidence of fear and not truth. Therefore, this is unsupportive to your ascension. Spirit knows that the energy of love is always your truth, and claiming accountability and taking the steps necessary for healing is an expression of love to yourself.

CHAPTER 9

Vulnerability and Ego Development

"The world is full of people who have stopped listening to themselves or have listened only to their neighbors to learn what they ought to do, how they ought to behave, and what the values are they should be living for."

- Joseph Campbell

As spirit, prior to our human birth, we choose the conditions and circumstances that will both inspire and challenge us toward becoming the highest version of ourselves. And then, as humans, we make choices moment to moment which will define our Earthly path and existence. Sometimes this is in alignment with our truth and sometimes it is not. But it is all a part of our individual process.

For whatever we choose or make of our lives, the opportunity exists for all people to fulfill their own unique higher purpose. Connected to our path of growth and ascension includes many varied relationships – parents, family, and many more. Of these, our childhood relationships are likely the most impactful, because we are receiving energy and training from others at a time when we are most vulnerable and dependent for our survival.

How we perceived our childhood has likely had a great impact on how we have learned to view and value ourselves. As we are able to be more accountable for our own energy and awareness, our job is to transcend that which does not serve our highest truth. This pertains to our ego training and disempowering beliefs. In other words, it is up to US to elevate our consciousness. This was never the job of our parents, or any other person.

As adults, while we may have felt disempowered by our childhood, our responsibility is to accept, understand, and then transform from our experiences. We can choose to retain our negativity and ignore the possibility of a higher truth and purpose, and simply continue to exist in the false perception and lower energy of ego (fear). However, since this does not serve your purpose of spiritual growth and evolution, this will never be satisfying or fulfilling. Instead, we must awaken to our truth and develop a practice of loving ourselves enough to learn from all that we have designed and attracted. This is the choice to live enlightened, with respect to our past relationships.

Regarding our childhood, we may have felt primarily loved, supported, and encouraged. Or we might have felt abandoned, ignored, and abused. At times we likely perceived each of these conditions, within our immature minds and underdeveloped awareness.

We absorbed the energy from our caregivers, and from the various other personalities and qualities that were attached to our unique path. In human terms, our perceptions were based upon a very limited understanding of our truth, or the truth of the others around us. This seems reasonable for children, yet this problem persists into adulthood for many people.

We relied upon other people to essentially fulfill all of our needs. From our perspective, that was their primary purpose. Of course we now know that they had much more to deal with in their life other than just satisfying us. From the standpoint of meeting our needs for physical and psychological wellness, we had little choice but to depend on our parents and others. Regarding our spiritual understanding, we likely were not taught or shown higher wisdom. And either way, we would need a substantial amount of mature awareness in order to accept this wisdom.

There is no doubt that we learn and experience a great deal in our formative years, both from the standpoint of nature and nurture. There are countless life paths and circumstances or conditions of a human childhood. I am not going to attempt to detail particular paths of healing for each, nor am I comparing or ranking them in terms of difficulty. I have compassion for all paths, and all paths lead to the healing and evolution of the individual. This is why we designed our path for spiritual growth and not necessarily for human comfort.

I am promoting the concept that from whatever your background, you may heal and transcend to a more enlightened path. Therefore, all people matter equally. In truth, while our human circumstances may look very different, everyone will likely experience challenges on one level or another in human terms. Regardless of our differences, our highest purpose is to integrate our spirituality into our humanity, to elevate our consciousness and share our light and love with all beings.

Again, we have chosen the particulars of our life path, which include certain other human souls in whom we will share at least a part of our journey. Our family relationships become our most intense and impactful teaching. This is because much of the lessons are received while we are quite vulnerable from a human standpoint. And this becomes our initial view and belief about our life path. Additionally, most people will maintain some connection to family members throughout a large portion of their lifetime. Therefore, there is continual opportunity for growth and support regarding our interaction with these people. Whether you are 5 years old or 65 (if you still interact with parents) you will be energetically impacted by their words or actions.

The family connection is so powerful that we are affected by both their presence and their absence, by the things they do or don't do for us, and even by the way in which we perceive their approval or disapproval. We have developed a high level of expectation that they will fulfill our needs on some level, and in some form this continues throughout our lives. We

63

start out in this vulnerable state whereby we must be "taken care of" for all of our basic needs. And this also bleeds into the fulfillment of our emotional needs as well.

Within our internal development we will compare our upbringing and the qualities of those who raise us, to our expectations of how we think things "should" be. The basis for this comparison comes from all that we observe from others, and from the mere fact that we believe that it is their job to always help us. In other words, if I have a problem, someone in my family is obligated to make it all better. Worse yet is when adults still blame their family for their problems. Obviously, under the weight of these expectations and judgments everyone will fall short. This immature perspective is based in ego delusion and not truth.

Having only been the recipient of care, we have little or no conception (or concern) of what other people are really experiencing. We don't really know what our family is doing for us, or what their particular sacrifices or challenges may be. Perhaps a parent is not as present or supportive as you would like, and you feel abandoned. Or maybe their version of being present consisted primarily of judging or controlling you. There are a myriad of ways in which we can feel dissatisfied with our childhood and by extension ourselves.

Therein lays the real problem. All that we experience and notice in the world (from our standpoint) is registered and recorded in our brain according to how it impacts us. Our ego nature translates this information into our value. Not our true value, but our perception of value. It wants to be continually approved and validated by others. This information is not objective data, but instead, false energy that has attached to our self-image and self-worth.

Of course, this is all beyond the ability of our parents or anyone else to control. They are likely doing the best they can within their own delusion. And so it goes, on and on. This ego monster that typically defines human behavior and beliefs must be tamed. This is nearly impossible to do as a child. And while challenging, it must be done as an adult. This is the only way to shift and elevate our consciousness and that of humanity.

The higher truth is that you are on your own unique life path as part of your overall spirit journey. And the same is equally true for all other people, even your parents and other family members. Ego development is the current natural condition of the world. Yet, it is delusion and not truth because it determines everything only from our lower identity and personal perspective. And the central concern is, "Are other people making me feel happy, satisfied, secure, and cared for?"

At the time of this writing, I have two very young grandsons. Of course, within their current life they will rightfully maintain this view. They have no choice. The problem is that through this ego development, the absence of higher truth, and our own lack of accountability, most adults have retained this same mantra.

They are still expecting other people to do things for them that only they can do for themselves. Through spiritual awareness and healing we may expand our perspective to fully understand our truth and responsibility for our own wellness. And even while we cannot heal others, we may be considerate and supportive to their higher truth. This is the true meaning of transcending relationships.

CHAPTER 10
Time to Transcend
Parental Guidance

*"We are not held back by the love we didn't receive in the past,
but by the love we're not extending in the present."*

- Marianne Williamson

The term transcending means to "rise above" or "go beyond." As we advance physically, mentally, emotionally and spiritually, we are meant to transcend our childhood perceptions. In other words, assuming that our life path extends into adulthood, where we start out is not meant to be our final destination in maturity or evolution. It is time to release the dependence upon parental approval and guidance. Connect to your higher truth and claim your power to choose that which is most loving and supportive for yourself.

Release the energy of insecurity, sensitivity, anger, blame, or other negative emotion you are still holding as an adult, that plagued you as a child. These energies may be poisoning your current perception of reality, and even the quality of your relationships. As we recognize our own accountability for our life, it is irresponsible not to honor our truth. As significant as our upbringing seems to us (for better or worse), you have the capability to heal, grow, and evolve. And as part of your unique life path, this is a responsibility that holds a key for you.

Certainly as a child it would be difficult to accept all of this with the higher understanding it warrants. Depending upon the level of consciousness of your parents you may have absorbed a false identity that has been very disempowering. Rather than making this an indictment on them, endeavor go release and forgive them completely, through higher wisdom and consciousness. Parents are people in need of healing and growth as well. Judging them for their actions based on fear and delusion only further attracts you to this energy within yourself.

Enlightenment is all about facilitating your own healing. And the only useful goal is to begin to discharge the negative energy that you have attached to before you knew your power. You are completely authorized, as a Divine Being living your human experience, to determine your own greatest path. This is always best done in an expression of love, as opposed to disrespect and defiance.

The truth is that parents typically instruct and encourage us to live our lives according to their truth, or at least their perception of truth. While they want us to succeed, it is usually according to their definition of success. For the most part they are doing this with loving intention. However, as we evolve as humans, we may recognize many of the past standards and beliefs as based in fear. You likely have a very different path and purpose than your parents (and certainly your grandparents). Therefore, this form of guidance may be disempowering and unsupportive.

Because of our past vulnerability and the ego development of our youth, our parents tend to hold a position of authority throughout our lives. We crave their approval and guidance because we are unsure or untrusting of our own truth. As always, our ego attempts to hold us in fear, which is due to the separation from our Authentic Self.

It now becomes imperative to connect to our truth as a priority toward facilitating trust in our own unique path and purpose. We have a choice to either heal and grow, or remain stuck in the negative energies of false perception. As is always the case for enlightenment, through your free will you will be required to choose love or fear. When you decide to honor your higher truth you are actually electing to love yourself. And this leads to loving all others as well.

However, when you continue to dishonor yourself by abdicating your responsibility for your own life, you create disharmony and dissatisfaction energetically. The longer you are attempting to live anyone else's truth, the greater your disconnection from Spirit. Accordingly, you are not in alignment with your Authentic Self. No matter whose approval you are attempting to garner, you are not fulfilling your highest purpose, and therefore, not living a fulfilling, authentic life.

In order to find your greatest fulfillment on this spiritual/human journey, you are meant to discover and trust your own truth. In this light, honoring your truth is not the same as dishonoring your parents. They may or may not be equipped to outwardly express this; yet, on a deeper level of their being, they know this to be true. Typically, as you become more secure and powerful within your own inner healing, others (including parents) will become more accepting and supportive.

As an adult you make your own choices. You can always choose to solicit advice or guidance from your parents or anyone else. In doing so, be aware of maintaining your inner power. Be accountable for both your choices and the results. Other people are simply offering their viewpoint, so be prepared to receive information that feels supportive or unsupportive, encouraging or critical. But work to remain unattached to their energy, and connected to your own.

Be mindful in whom you confide in matters that may test your vulnerability or inner strength. As we are stretching and growing to live a more expanded and authentic life, we press up against our own inner fear often. At times you will feel a strong desire to share your feelings, experiences, and progress. Do your best to make sure that the person in whom you are confiding has your highest trust. Over-sharing to people who do not understand your higher vision can deplete your best energy and redirect you to fear. If you ask for advice and you receive wisdom that resonates as truth for you, be grateful. And if not, be gracious and kind, but do not feel obligated to use their advice.

If you are still involved with your parents, then appreciate, accept, and honor them for who they are. You never need to be defiant, disrespectful, or otherwise engage in a power struggle. To do so would mean that you are living in fear instead of love. Release the need to prove yourself right or them wrong. This is just another way of expressing fear as you seek their approval.

We must always strive for empowering relationships, and this includes family. The extent to which you honor each other will dictate the quality of the relationship. If you have different points of view and interests, but are still able respect each other, then you can maintain a wonderful experience together. If instead, you are continually criticized and disrespected while living your highest truth, then you may choose to diminish or discontinue your sharing of time together. You have the power to choose, and the responsibility for your wellness.

There typically will be some natural conflict or incompatibility between parents and children. This is not just an unreasonable burden or cause for unhappiness. In truth it serves a higher purpose. It is actually useful toward facilitating our own inner healing, growth, and ascension. It becomes a lifelong opportunity to honor our truth in the face of opposition. And this is because we are required to transcend our perception of vulnerability and insufficiency versus those who initially held authority over us.

This is a factor in the agreement we made with each other as Spirit. The specific qualities and challenges to be experienced were designed into our life plan. This form of teaching may at times be unpleasant or even harmful on the human/ego level. Yet, once we transcend our lower based identity and connect to higher truth, we may develop an inner strength and conviction to honor our true self. This leads directly to the fulfillment of our higher purpose.

This takes great intention and courage for most of us. The easier path is to succumb to your parent's desires, and then to whomever else comes along after them to control you. This will never be fulfilling, for it is not your true purpose. It prevents you from fully shining your light into the world. And we all need your light.

Better to understand this early in life, or you may spend decades looking for the wrong things on the wrong path. In any case, whenever we are able to awaken it is of tremendous value. Know that even as adults, other than regarding the most enlightened of parents, you will be constantly challenged to abandon your path for theirs. Love them anyway, because their intentions are likely pure, but hold fast to your truth.

When you receive words from others that are accepting and supportive, offer your appreciation. This both supports their wellness and is confirmation that you are more fully honoring yourself. This represents the quality of love, and is a gift. You may now be further encouraged to persevere in the fulfillment of your purpose.

Sometimes a parent (or others of significant influence) expresses their displeasure with your path or offers guidance that in no way is in alignment with your truth. In response we may become defensive, depending on how tactfully their expression is offered. But in any case, it does not feel good to the ego. Additionally, there may be further disappointment in the lack of acceptance from others.

Yet in truth, they are reflecting back to us our inner energy that is still holding some doubt or fear about our path and purpose. This most often shows up when we are attempting significant changes in the direction of honoring our truth. Again, this is an act of tremendous courage. Naturally we feel vulnerable having moved away from the more comfortable path of striving to please others. Therefore, we are a target for fear-based beliefs.

71

Even as you recognize this as a challenge to your ego, be encouraged that you now understand this for what it is. First, it is evidence that you are developing higher awareness. This is a wonderful opportunity for you to trust yourself – to continue to grow and evolve. With this higher awareness you may work to deal with this disturbance on an inner level, where it actually is coming from. It may serve you well in confirming that you are now living your unique life and fulfilling your special purpose. Use affirmations as often as possible to reinforce the transformation of your inner dialog. It also is a reminder that you are fully responsible for offering love and healing to yourself and remaining non-attached to the fearful energy of others.

Always focus on yourself first. Be the best YOU that you can be. That is always enough. You will not change your parents, nor should you. As you gain greater inner strength and empowerment you will become a force that is less likely to be subjected to parental critique. So work on developing your energetic awareness, and continue to define your greatest path for the fulfillment of your true purpose.

CHAPTER 11
Some Truth about Parenting

"Children are educated by what the grown-up is and not by his talk."

- Carl Jung

While we are relatively unconscious, we are not functioning within our highest love in any aspect of our life. Within the context of family, this lower energetic level of awareness, which is based in fear, can be harmful, delusional, and disempowering. Therefore, it is imperative that parents become more enlightened and concerned about the influence of their expressions of energy upon their children.

Conscious Parenting is such a critical issue to the evolution of humanity. I am writing a book in the *On the Enlightened Path* series about this topic. But the truth remains that wherever we are in our journey as child, adolescent, or adult, we are experiencing the path we chose for purposes of our own healing, growth, and evolution. As I have stated, my awareness has taught me that we have chosen our parents and family as partners on our spiritual/human path. Therefore, while they play a significant role in our human development, we are never justified in abdicating our responsibility for our own wellness.

A great truth about parenting is that it is a great opportunity for service, and not an entitlement of ownership. Our children have been placed in our care, yet their life belongs to them. When we look at our history, this has been lost on humanity.

At times, it seems that parents (intentionally or unintentionally) have had children for purposes that served themselves. If it supported their livelihood, children may have been thought of as workers or property. Or maybe we derived some personal value in requiring them to live out our dreams. Our children are not possessions, and they are not inferior to us. They may be more vulnerable and weaker physically, yet spiritually, they are at least as powerful as you.

More parents need to understand the solemn connection, responsibility, and value in supporting the healthy growth and development of their children. This often does not mean that they don't love them, or that they are not doing their best. Instead, they may simply be too unhealthy or otherwise ill-equipped within their own existence, to be conscious parents.

As opposed to a general criticism of parenting, my purpose is to call upon an awakening. What would be more empowering to the evolution of humanity but for parents to evolve? Until we can shift to a greater understanding of, and accessibility to, our inner love and power, we cannot teach or imprint this upon our children. Enlightened parents raise loving, empowered people. And of course, the reverse is true as well.

If you are a parent, no matter what reason caused you to have children, I hope that you will shift and awaken to the tremendous responsibility and opportunity that you have. And by the way, this pertains as much to men as it does to women. These Divine humans/Souls have chosen you to teach, guide, and support them, and this must be looked upon as a privilege. One way or another they will live their life and fulfill their Soul's purpose. However, you have the opportunity to help them realize their greatest potential, by supporting them to fully love, honor, and value their truth.

Of course good parenting is one of the most difficult jobs. The level of patience, selflessness, kindness, attentiveness, along with the time and energy it takes, is enormous. This is a lifetime commitment and an exercise in unconditional love. All of this is required while you are dealing with your own issues of wellness, relationships, career, etc. Why is it that the most important jobs pay the least money? Oh that's right, because true value has little or nothing to do with money.

When we live unconscious, selfish, and immature lives, we may go into this most important role unprepared. Or if we function under the delusion that our children are here to serve us (because that was the attitude of past unenlightened generations) we may ignore their higher needs for emotional wellness. In either case, our children will suffer, and we will likely stunt their development toward realizing their true value, worthiness, and self-love.

Of course, when we are unable to support our children in this way, we help create their need for inner healing later in life. We adversely affect their well-being as adults, including their relationship choices and experiences. Again, at whatever age or stage of your life, if you are a parent you must awaken to the inner transformation that leads to your greatest life and contribution. From this place, even if your children are now adults, elevate your consciousness to be loving and supportive in the way that THEY need, for THEIR greatest development and wellness.

Maybe your parents were unprepared to tackle this extraordinary job. They likely did their best. Even though this is truth, it's not much consolation in most cases. Still, you could not control their level of consciousness or ability to parent. You must accept the training that you got. In the previous chapter I wrote about the need to release and transcend the influence of your parents now that you are an adult. This is the only thing that you have control over that will support your best life.

Regardless of the quality of parenting you received or offered, parents are human, and mistakes will be made. Do not expect perfection from them or yourself. As much as possible, be responsible for finding your own solutions to truth and happiness independent of your family. We are all on a path of healing, growing, and evolution. This means that we are to live, be, and do, in a higher capacity than those who came before us. Once we are more conscious, we can learn from past mistakes, and create a greater present and future.

You must understand and accept that the parenting you received was about them and not about you. You must also accept that you, and not they, are ultimately responsible for your well-being. In both cases you must know on a deep level that you are loved, valued, and whole, and that you have a higher purpose in this life. These are internal qualities of Spirit that are your higher truth.

What can you learn on the human level? You have seen countless examples of how to communicate and interact with others. You have seen the result of where people place their values. You have been shown a perspective that judges other people who may think or look differently than you. You have witnessed the degree of effort people make regarding many important issues around survival, achievement, and lifestyle.

Some of what you were taught will support you in living your unique enlightened life. Many other things will not resonate as your truth, when connected to your higher identity. So stop focusing on judging your parents, instead, honor your truth and integrate the lessons that best serve you. The overall shifting and evolving in the world is to create more love and support for all people.

We are ascending to love, replacing the control of fear. There are still plenty of people holding on to fear as a way of life. But I believe that new generations will have no use for this fear-based judgment that separates and devalues people. There is simply no good reason to carry on the fearful expressions of past generations; the thoughts, words, and actions that have manifested as hate, judgement, prejudice, greed, anger, ignorance, insecurity, materiality, etc. This is the reason that negative human conditions have been so slow to evolve. And this is why conscious parenting is so critical for purposes of raising more enlightened generations. Parents must teach love and Unity Consciousness to their young children.

CHAPTER 12
Early Challenges that Create Growth

*"Character cannot be developed in ease and quiet.
Only through experience of trial and suffering can the soul be
strengthened, ambition inspired, and success achieved."*

- Helen Keller

Conflicting Energies and Traits

Included with our unique gifts, abilities, interests, and passion, are certain personality traits and temperament. We are likely to have significant family members with the opposite qualities. This creates the consequence of some natural conflicts in our early relationships as a direct result of our pre-incarnation choices. As a youth in our human/ego state this sometimes creates tension that can feel very disempowering and frustrating. In this chapter I will explain a higher truth about these early conflicts that may support your healing, growth, and ascension

Interestingly enough, this tension may provide one of our greatest growth opportunities. The challenge of these conflicting personalities will be experienced differently by different people. A child that is more naturally assertive may have an easier time developing their own identity than one who is more passive. However, they both will have an opportunity to ultimately receive what they need to learn about themselves. While the difficulty can be increased or lessened by the quality and consciousness of the parenting involved, in order to reach our highest potential we must overcome these early challenges at some point.

Did you think that it was just a coincidence that you are so different in so many ways from your parents? The truth is that from an early age we are given the opportunity to recognize and honor our truth. Through a wide range of encouraging support or inflammatory critiques, it is our purpose to discover our true self.

Part of the challenge is that all of this is immersed in the vulnerability and ego development that encompass our childhood and upbringing; therefore, we are particularly susceptible, at this early stage, to abandoning our truth and conforming to the will of our life teachers.

You may be a bit adventurous, active, forceful, outspoken, emotional, a risk taker, and extroverted. Yet one or more of your parents tends to be calm, controlled, quiet, measured, passive, habitual, and introverted. Or you may find that the qualities of parent/child work the other way around. There is also likely a difference in outward expression of our energy, stamina, and drive.

At this point it is not about good-bad, better-worse, conscious-unconscious. Our traits are perfectly designed for our purpose, and since it is imperative to pursue growth, we need not believe that we should be more like someone else. Always strive to be the best you that YOU can be.

So you grow up within a family unit and teaching that may not affirm your true higher nature. As always, when people are respectful, aware, kind, and supportive, we all may thrive within our own truth. Obviously this is the goal for all empowered relationships. Unfortunately this is often not the reality for many people.

Let's say that your nature is most supported in an environment that is more reserved, peaceful, and inwardly contemplative. You might have a parent who naturally functions in a more frantic-active state, and who verbalizes their energy and expectations in a very aggressive manner. You likely are not feeling supported in the integration of your truth into your humanity. In this case, you may feel disempowered, and even bullied. Not only that, you may develop a perception that in order to be valued at home (and in the world) you must act in ways that conform to this more forceful energy or behavior.

Your challenge is to identify and connect to your truth, in the face of this adversity. You must find your space of empowerment in whatever form, method, or activity supports you. This is a most important thing to learn, because you will encounter this conflicting energy from other people throughout your life. And the more prepared and developed you are in maintaining your best energy in these situations, the more loving, peaceful, and successful you will be.

Again, it works both ways. You may have a more active nature that wants to try to do many things. This is your natural expression. Yet your parents may be more settled, subdued, and less expressive about your more outwardly energetic interests. You feel unsupported in living your highest truth. And may actually feel ignored or abandoned, as you focus greatly on gaining their praise for your achievements. The answer is still the same; you must tailor your tools and methods to suit your unique perspective.

Our family relationships offer opportunities for healing and growth through the very nature of opposing forces of personality. We chose these specific circumstances and conditions, and with a higher understanding of this wisdom, we will be able to utilize our experiences to our benefit.

Otherwise, to position ourselves to be either offended or disempowered, is unsupportive and detrimental to our wellness. Until we learn to accept our truth as whole and perfect for our journey, we will struggle to honor ourselves. And as adults when we do not fully honor ourselves, we will attract more relationship teachers who reflect an unsupportive energy back to us. Of course, this is designed to teach us to awaken, but while unconscious, it typically brings more suffering.

When we believe that our truth is inadequate for worldly survival and success, we will feel like we are inferior or missing something vital. In this case we may continually look at others as having what we need to make us whole. This is why there is so much unhappiness and dissatisfaction in people's lives. We have been searching without – to heal the delusion within. It is false to think that anyone else is better equipped to live YOUR best life. And it is a tragedy to chase someone else's dreams.

This is the basis and necessity for awakening to your own Authentic Self in this human life. Because our view and value have most often been placed on external conditions and teachers, we often will miss the truth of our path and purpose. Therefore, this is an inner pursuit. You have been learning all of the ways you are supposed to do things, and all of the things that you are supposed to want in your life. Now you recognize that you are required to make intentional choices and an on-going effort to listen and follow your own inner knowing.

Depending upon your path, you may come to this understanding as a teenager or it may happen much later in life. Some people never find the light that obliterates these shadows. So transcending and overcoming a challenge is a process of healing and growth that supports your evolution. Had you simply chosen humans/Souls with complete compatibility, you would not have been required to facilitate such a transformation and commitment to yourself.

Within this level of healing, these challenges of our childhood may effectively prepare us for adulthood, and the fulfillment of our purpose. We may learn to love, honor, and know ourselves on a deeper level that is more empowering to us. Additionally, we have gained experience in dealing with various contradictory personality traits in a positive and healthy way. If we can do this from our higher awareness, we can be more effective within our interactions, while maintaining our inner wellness.

Difficult Human Challenges

The section above will likely be pertinent to all people, however, some of us have chosen human conditions that are more extreme than others. Within the context that we choose our life circumstances to fit the higher purpose of our Soul, there may likely be any number of reasons why one might pick a particularly challenging childhood. In using your highest awareness in connection to your Authentic Self, this would be a valuable thing for you to understand; though it is likely that this may not be available until you have some distance, experience, and teaching in higher wisdom.

Applying the keys to *Mastering Your Life* will support you in your healing and transformation. Higher wisdom may set you upon an empowered path that supports you in fulfilling your unique purpose in a satisfying human experience. Plus, you now become a new standard and model for future generations. Therein may lay your higher truth for choosing this path. While neglecting to examine this aspect of your life could lead to generational dysfunction, disadvantage, and victimhood.

I would never discount anyone's particular experience of pain and suffering within their childhood. No one can fully know how things impact others, so we always must allow for compassion. However, my greatest focus is to support you in understanding this dynamic on a higher level, and to encourage you to choose to honor yourself by shifting and transforming your present energy and experience.

Maybe there was abuse, abandonment, addictions, poverty, discrimination, etc. We can use these negative circumstances to stay stuck in a disempowering perspective of our life, whereby this becomes our identity and a reason to justify our dissatisfaction or lack of success. In addition to the circumstance itself, there may be many people encouraging us to stay down because they are not ready to transform. However, while your challenges to overcome these conditions may be more difficult than some others, you are here because your Spirit chose this path. And if your Spirit chose this, then your mission somehow involves dealing with and transcending your challenges.

In transforming your life you add greater light into the world. You have abundant value to contribute while living your truth and offering your loving presence to all. The standard is always to be self-determined. In the assessment of your success it matters not what others have or do. You may rise to the level of self-sufficiency, conscious parenting, a valued worker, or even a position in which you positively influence many. There is no ranking, as your best life is always enough.

We may find that we have a particular sensitivity over our childhood conditions. From an elevated view your Spirit may have chosen this path as a catalyst for you to offer higher service into the world by supporting others similarly afflicted by their challenges. You will have an experiential understanding of the need to assist or guide others. As you transcend to your greatest empowerment and love, your strength and truth will be of enormous benefit to many. In a world that is elevating in consciousness and transforming from all types of delusion and fear-based behavior, this service is extremely valuable to all.

Your early life circumstances were chosen by you as Spirit for the higher purpose of evolution. Now, as an adult, you have the capability of choosing how you will heal and transform from these conditions in order to fulfill this purpose. You must move past the false belief that others "owe" you anything, or that your life is "unfair." No one will heal and transform for you, we are each responsible for ourselves.

It is not about undoing anything from the past, or "righting the wrongs." You must accept that your path is unique from all others, and that the family conditions that were so negative are now in the past. You can only affect your quality of life and wellness here in the present. This is where your true power lies.

You are fully accountable for creating your best life. Choose to accept the higher identity of your Authentic Self, and know that you are valuable and here on purpose. Integrating this truth through awareness in the present moment is empowering. Release your attachment to the fearful false beliefs that ego has fed your mind all of these years. Find the loving energy of your inner truth, and thereby, the compassion to release and forgive those people who mistreated you due to their inherent unconsciousness.

What you are releasing is the attachment to the negative energy that still binds you. They were in need of healing and were unable to awaken to their higher truth. Don't make the same mistakes they did, which leads to the mistreatment of yourself and others. Instead, choose to offer the love and support to yourself that they could not offer to themselves or you.

How you choose to express your energy will directly impact your life now, including your present relationships and experiences. Utilize the lessons from your youth to decide upon the conditions that now will serve your highest good. Be empowered to find the freedom of living your life in fulfillment of your greatest gifts, qualities, and passion. When utilized in this way you may offer yourself the energetic healing that you expected, but never received, from others. Within this awakening process you are transcending the perception of suffering that ego has made your reality.

You may now shift to a new reality that is based in spiritual truth. Be accountable for your own wellness. Always strive to live in your light regardless of the opinion of those who have not yet recognized their own. There is great joy and freedom in knowing that your job is to stay on a path that honors you, and accepts others as they are.

CHAPTER 13

Learning Our Value in Intimate Relationships

"When you realize that nothing is lacking,
the whole world opens up to you."

- Lao Tzu

When it comes to our more intimate relationships, we have likely brought our vulnerability, ego, and false identity with us. And as younger adults we also bring a lack of worldly experience. Without a level of awakening to our truth, this is a pretty challenging place from which to create empowering relationships.

We are insecure and ignorant about our true value and potential for conscious decision making. However, if we choose to engage in enlightened living, we will make great strides in overcoming these challenges. Otherwise, many people often live their entire adult lives going from one bad relationship to the next.

Our ego draws us into situations, experiences, and relationships that, while initially exciting, are fraught with danger, from the standpoint of our wellness. Some people develop an addiction to this drama. We will encounter many chances to either honor or dishonor ourselves. Some choices lead to setbacks and suffering that we would have wished to avoid, yet this is the path of learning for those who are still unconscious.

At first we are learning through trial and error because we are inexperienced. Eventually, however, we are supposed to acquire the wisdom available from these lessons, and then make relationship choices in a more conscious manner. Yet, when we still have a false and disempowering self-image, we may likely ignore the signs that should guide our experiences to happier outcomes. Due to a lack of understanding about our own value, we attempt to "manage" our affairs by settling for less and then trying to manipulate others to meet our needs. Inevitably, when they are unable to do this, we blame them and lament our choices.

We may find people to date simply because of physical attraction or because they are available and interested. This may be a fun and lighthearted connection. Or it can turn more intense and heavy, depending upon the lessons you are attracting. However, all ego attachment is delusion and ultimately unfulfilling and unsatisfying.

Within the media, both men and women are continuously manipulated with images and messages about what is attractive or sexually satisfying; two significant drivers for the human condition. Therefore, this has become quite overvalued in our society. In the name of commerce and greed, you are a target. Whether it is the continual advertising of products to help your "performance," or body images that are unattainable to 99% of humanity, big business is targeting your ego. And because of this input we not only have a diminished self-image, but we may be seeking relationship partners based upon the physical qualities we now believe are so vital.

This is all part of the ego indoctrination of society that impacts our energetic expressions, which negatively affect our personal relationships. It attacks our true value by causing us to judge ourselves and others on the basis of arbitrary physical qualities. Of course, everyone is taught to desire youth and beauty. And this is wonderful for what it is – temporary and subjective. If we are living unconsciously, unaware of our energy, all of this attention directed toward our vanity can serve to diminish our self-worth and value.

This is not a good/bad, right/wrong thing. However, it is not in alignment with your Authentic Self, and may be unsupportive of your wellness and the creation of transcendent relationships. For the sake of enlightened living, we all need to be particularly concerned with developing our most "attractive" inner qualities in order to attract these qualities in others. This supports our overall wellness.

When we are so focused upon our physical nature (and not our spiritual identity), we make many decisions based upon the intensity of physical attraction. Oftentimes, we may make some form of commitment to a relationship based upon these factors. Later we realize that there is little or no true match on a level that supports our higher life purpose or wellness.

If we are lacking in self-love, it will always show up in our relationships. And the greatest sign of identifying with ego instead of Spirit is the denial of your true loving nature and value. We may "settle" for someone simply because they show enough interest in us. Or we will promote an over-confident version of ourselves and then sabotage the relationship before the other person gets a chance to see what we really think of ourselves. Here you may find the serial cheaters, liars, and manipulators. Of course, all of these negative qualities and conditions are equally true for both men and women.

When we understand our innate value and purpose, we will honor ourselves enough to recognize the potential impact that another person has on our energy and wellness. We will patiently take the time to get to know this person on a deeper more real level. And then we can decide if we wish to offer them our highest love and companionship. If you desire to connect on the level of partnership, it becomes imperative that that they "add to the light of your already-whole and valuable life."

In the determination of a partnership type of relationship, you should consider all aspects of your life – career, family, money, lifestyle, intimacy, faith, and much more. If it is a marriage, or the intent is to otherwise enter a long-term relationship, together you must also consider your future for growth and expansion, individually and collectively. Not that we can always know enough to ensure long-term success; I am merely offering the reasonable communication process one would undertake while consciously creating an empowered partnership.

So how many of you have been conscious enough to make the wise, empowering selection of a spouse or partner in this manner? Yah, me neither. In truth, I was often not in an enlightened space while making relationship choices in the past. I was functioning within the control of ego that attracted the experiences I needed in order to learn my value and to recognize my own power. Therefore, I did the best I could, but ultimately I needed to learn through suffering – like most of us.

I now take full responsibility for attracting my relationships and for maintaining the connection with my Authentic Self that supports my highest good within all aspects of my life. But there is nothing like an intimate relationship to show you (and others) what you really think of yourself. Sometimes I was the one who ended the relationship, and sometimes she did – either way can be painful. Occasionally, you have a mutual ending that is relatively friendly and peaceful.

If you are "lucky" you will experience a relationship that finally gets your attention, and directs you toward an awakening. And if you are "wise" you will not need to repeat this experience. This one is not the happy ending. This is the relationship that will kick your ass. Through the intense suffering and transition you will not consider yourself lucky. In fact you may be forced to question your value and purpose on a deep level. My dear friends, this is a true soul mate connection, which is far from the Disney fairytale romance you hoped for.

Ultimately this relationship offers the potential for healing, growth, and transformation leading to your spiritual awakening. You will be humbled and broken down, but apparently this is what you needed in order to learn a new truth – the truth about your higher value and purpose. Had you not needed this, on the level of energy you would not have attracted it.

Are you going to overcome and transcend, or are you going to curl up and die? Are you finally going to learn to love yourself and all others, or are you going to remain the victim and mistrust the world? The choice is always yours, and your Spirit has been guiding you to choose love.

This is another great example of the difference between our true spiritual purpose and our human desire for comfort, ease, and security. Learn to appreciate your darkest times and most challenging relationships as part of your process to enlightenment. You attracted this in support of your potential for healing, growth, and ascension. In order to accomplish this, you must separate their human actions from the value of the lessons they forced you to face. When we are unconscious we all may act inappropriately, yet this does not diminish our higher spiritual identity.

We are given the tremendous opportunity in our human journey to awaken to our truth. And relationships offer a wonderful occasion to do just that. Are we going to finally recognize the value these experiences offer toward teaching us about healing and loving ourselves unconditionally? Or are we going to continue to attract partners that will reflect the most unloving qualities back to us, time after time? I am not expressing criticism; I am offering that this is a choice that only you can make for yourself. Our energy will always move us in the direction of evolution, we cannot avoid this. So for the sake of your human satisfaction and fulfillment, choose to learn and grow through inner love.

Look at the partners you have attracted in the past, and even who you are attracting now. If you are honest and willing to be accountable for yourself, you will awaken to a great truth. What is the energy you are putting out into the world when attempting to fulfill your desires? And as far as that goes, what are these desires you seek to fill? If we want a mate or partner, what is our inner motivation and outer expression?

How you are able to answer these questions will likely determine the quality of the experience you have in your more intimate relationships. This will offer an enlightened view of who you are likely to attract. Our focus must first be on our own healing and wellness, if we hope to attract someone who is healthy and loving. We can then love ourselves enough to be responsible for choosing relationships that are empowering. We love our self and we are choosing to offer true love to another. And until we love our true self, we will not be able to fully honor and love our partner.

If our primary reasons are for anything other than this, we are coming from lack and will attract a similarly unhealthy partner. Do not blame the partner. They are here to serve you (energetically) by showing you your delusion and disconnection from Spirit. If you are simply displeased with your life because you feel you are missing some quality you think is required from another person, then you will attract someone to mirror your need for inner healing. Now you will have other issues to deal with, in addition to the energy deficit that caused this relationship.

Many of our human needs are temporary, as energy is constantly moving and changing. At times we all feel lonely, isolated, bored, etc. in our life. We do not need a "lifetime" commitment and a grand gesture to resolve our temporary loneliness. Our growth in connection to our Authentic Self will support us in finding satisfying and fulfilling alternatives most of the time. Plus, we must learn to honor our alone time as well, and to be more patient and present.

Another ego problem for many people is that they feel the burden of societal expectations. This says that to not be partnered means something is wrong with you. When your true value comes from within, and not from other people, you will recognize this is a completely ridiculous concept. In truth we can spend quality time with people in various capacities beyond the one intimate partner. The key to our happiness always lies within.

Utilize the great lessons from your past intimate relationships. You have experienced caring, joy, sharing, contribution to another, disappointment, sadness, anger, and unhappiness. You likely have felt every human emotion at some point. Explore these experiential lessons in a more objective way. Determine your greatest need and desire for inner healing and wellness, and then decide upon the higher qualities that you now wish share and receive from an intimate partner. This should be most supportive to your understanding of your best empowered life.

CHAPTER 14
Recognizing Co-Dependency

"Love gives naught but itself and takes naught but from itself. Love possesses naught nor would it be possessed; for love is sufficient unto love."

- Kahlil Gibran

I believe that everyone is familiar with the concept of co-dependency. However, many people don't think that it applies to them; but I say that all relationships are on some level co-dependent. This is because while human we are never free from ego, never fully connected to Spirit (or higher consciousness). Therefore, on some level we will all succumb to our attachment to other people as a way to meet our own needs and desires. Living enlightened at least supports us in minimizing our dependencies by facilitating our inner healing and wellness.

The customary understanding of co-dependency is when one partner is in some way controlling the other, while the other is allowing themselves to be controlled. However, in truth, there are aspects and times in our relationships when either person is the controller or controlled. This energy exchange is based in the ego delusion that tells us that we are not whole and completely worthy of love on our own.

I control you because I am not strong enough to allow you to be yourself, and I don't want to be alone. I allow myself to be controlled because I believe that I am unworthy of more loving treatment, and I don't want to be alone. Of course, the controller feels more powerful, which is what they are missing inside; and the controlled is expressing their inner powerlessness. They are two sides of the same coin. Some will try to justify this as duty or the fulfillment of some obligation that is more important than their happiness. But ultimately it is a reflection of one who is detached from their Authentic Self. And since we always have free will, ultimately they are choosing a relationship based in fear and not love.

In this scenario no one is happy or fulfilled within their spiritual truth, and they are likely suffering within their humanity as well. The best they can hope for is the ego satisfaction of temporary "wins," or moments of peaceful coexistence. Neither person is primarily connected to their Authentic Self, because if they were, two things would be true. First, they likely would never have attracted the other person to begin with; and two, if they did, they would not continue to endure such a dysfunctional and disempowering relationship.

Many co-dependent relationships are steeped in unconscious ego control. They may be so far removed from their Authentic Self that they are not even aware that such a thing exists. Some involve addictions and abusive behavior that always entail suffering and the obvious need for inner healing. Both participants are vying to have their ego needs met by the other, and of course, both are finding great disappointment that this is not happening. Neither is being sufficiently accountable for their wellness.

In these cases you will find two disempowered people fulfilling very dysfunctional energy attractions. For many it becomes necessary for them to disengage from the relationship in order to focus on their own inner healing. This may take great courage and self-awareness. There is a sincere need to awaken to their higher truth, and they likely must rise above childhood challenges and other past relationship difficulties in this process.

If we are honoring and loving ourselves and each other, we can experience a mutual dependency that is supportive to the higher goals and desires of each. We are each responsible for our own wellness and the fulfillment of our life path. However, we are choosing to do this together, from inner strength and not outer desperation. Our inner needs are met, therefore we have the capacity to accept and honor our partner just as they are.

Since we are always in the process of living enlightened, we will continue to share energy in each present moment. In the times when we temporarily go unconscious, we will be required to learn through challenging energy exchanges. So we will continue to be teachers as well as partners. As long as we do this with love, we will support our growth and wellness together. This is a healthy relationship that is based in love as opposed to attachment.

CHAPTER 15

Divorce Is a Transition, Not a Failure

*"Out of clutter, find simplicity. From discord, find harmony.
In the middle of difficulty lies opportunity."*

- Albert Einstein

From the perspective of non-attachment, divorce is merely the legal ending of a marriage. Of course, marriage is a legalized relationship. Beyond the legal status, on a human level there may be a great upheaval of energy, family ties, emotion, lifestyle, finances, etc. Therefore, great awareness and wisdom should be applied when deciding to get divorced, whether or not this was the case regarding the decision to get married.

Typically, divorce (or any ending) was not the intent when entering into the agreement to marry. So when it does end there is often great fear and disappointment. In addition to the many details and inconveniences that make divorce difficult, many have been conditioned to accept the burden of societal judgement – introducing shame. This only becomes an issue if we accept this external condition as our inner truth. The labeling of your experience as "failure" is unnecessary and unsupportive to your wellness. And it has no basis in higher truth.

Many have made marriage a moral or religious issue – this is based in fear and not love. I am not speaking about where you choose to be married, only to the external approval or pressure of doing so. In addition to this being the basis for encouraging some to get married, it has also been the arbitrary excuse to restrict certain other people in our society from having the legal right to marry. I believe that this preponderance of fearful energy has played a significant role in creating our very high rate of divorce.

Besides the legal ramifications, marriage is a choice to experience a portion of our life path in combination with another individual. People make this choice all of the time, yet when it becomes legal (a marriage) and it ends, suddenly there is this negative connotation. This judgement is not in alignment with the true spiritual purpose of the union. Should you take the decision to get married seriously? Yes, absolutely. Does the act of getting married automatically make it a healthy, empowered relationship? No, of course not.

We agree to marry someone for a whole host of reasons. And this all represents our level of consciousness and understanding of our life path at the time. But our relationships are tools to facilitate our inner healing and growth, and we choose others based upon our energetic wellness versus this need for healing. So the decision to join together with another person for the remainder of your human life is rarely a sound choice based in wisdom, awareness, and knowing. Regardless of our intentions and vows, it is a commitment for an indeterminate amount of time. Sometimes it lasts, most of the time it doesn't, and that is just the nature of human relations.

In truth, people are doing their best to get their needs met, based on their understanding of this at a particular point in time. The more prepared and conscious they are, the better the chances for a satisfying match. More often the decision to get married is based on the temporary qualities of physical attraction, co-dependency, and an infatuation for certain qualities or traits. We may be neglecting to fully consider the issues of character and true compatibility which are most essential. And beyond this, some marriages are based in deception, manipulation, and coercion. Still, regardless of the motivations, this is a relationship you attracted energetically for the purposes of healing, growth, and evolution. Of course, this is true for all relationships, yet marriage typically adds a higher level of challenge and learning opportunities.

If the two partners are sufficiently connected to their love energy, they may certainly work through life's challenging issues together in a mutually supportive way. This is the marriage that may live up to its initial intentions. You know, "until death do us part." The life paths are aligned and the two people are willing and able to honor themselves and each other in a loving and healthy atmosphere.

Any marriage relationship that falls short of such a loving and conscious connection will likely take one of two paths. One, the couple decides to end the marriage by getting a divorce, though this may initially be sought by only one of the spouses. And two, they stay together. If the choice is to stay married, then once again, there are two possible scenarios: one, they each commit to working on their inner healing, together and separately; or two, they stay in a stagnant, dysfunctional arrangement that no longer serves the highest good for either partner.

It is likely that in all of the above cases the relationship in question was intended to be temporary and not lifelong. The true value and purpose of the connection was real, however, it was not supposed to be a lifetime commitment. If one must use the judgmental term of "failure," only the couple staying together while continuing to create suffering could be considered as such, and not the divorced couple. This is because, in staying together, they are choosing to dishonor their higher truth and purpose, and to be unsupportive in their own healing and wellness. And this choice is typically resonating from some form of inner fear.

Ending a challenging marriage does not make the relationship good or bad, it just is what it is. Labels are often unsupportive and delusional. Here are some better questions: Are you able to determine the true value and purpose of the connection? Can you further internalize this information in order to begin to formulate a process of deeper healing and wisdom, to support you in making more empowering choices in the future? This is called growth.

The human experiences may have been largely unpleasant, but on a spiritual level we created an opportunity to learn valuable lessons in love. Marriage is not meant to be a death sentence. When it ends it is certainly more complicated than ending a non-marriage relationship, but this is the consequence of making legal what on the level of energy was intended to be temporary.

Sometimes the couple has children together, and on that level there is an on-going mutual obligation, that comprises the extent of the relationship in the present and future. However this must become a new connection, one that honors each person individually from a distance, while jointly caring for the children. Use higher awareness and maturity to be accountable for yourself, and refrain from expressing ongoing negativity toward your kids other parent. This is so much healthier for them than subjecting them to an unsupportive and unloving home life. Release the fearful energy that convinces you to stay together for your children. It is likely a false and self-serving delusion.

What is true for the ending of most intimate relationships is nearly always true for a divorce – that we feel hurt, sad, guilty, embarrassed, and angry. We hold these negative emotions both toward ourselves and our partner. This may be a natural part of the mourning and healing process, but since it is based in fear, it prevents you from seeing your higher truth. You have an opportunity to awaken to your greatest love by taking responsibility for your wellness, so endeavor to shift to the truth of the matter and be encouraged and excited on your new path.

Usually there is some amount of goodness shared in even the most volatile relationships. However, that may have only strung you along by blocking your higher awareness, and this is not enough to justify the suffering that is the predominant quality of the relationship. Your instincts are likely correct, before your mind (or other people) introduce fear.

Better to recognize your true higher value and release your attachment to the disempowering and debilitating energy that is limiting your joy and potential. As always, you are here to live your unique human experience with great passion and purpose, you are not here to be demeaned or enslaved by a partner.

If you still have some fear and self-judgment around a divorce, begin to realize your higher identity. You are a spiritual being having a human experience, and not simply someone's spouse or partner. Accept that this is a relationship whose value has come and gone, even if there are still some caring and positive feelings. If your best life (and theirs) is moving you in a different direction than you must honor that.

Release your attachment to ego that holds thoughts of regret, resentment, or embarrassment. These are false energies that do not support your healing, growth, and ascension. Also release any negative energy toward your former partner. You do not have to condone anyone's hurtful actions. However, you are only penalizing yourself while attached to this energy. In short, be fully accountable for all of your past experiences in order to learn, heal, and transform into the enlightened space of choosing and living more wisely in the present.

Begin to focus on your own healing first, and use your greater awareness to consciously connect with people who support your higher self-love and value. You may decide to apply this enlightened view to attract a more empowering relationship, or you may choose (for now) to fully enjoy your wellness and freedom while single. In any case, focus more time and attention on the pursuits that bring fulfillment and add your light into the world. This is a great time to discover and walk YOUR enlightened path.

CHAPTER 16
7 Steps for Healing and Transformation

*"The most important thing is transforming our minds,
for a new way of thinking, a new outlook: we should
strive to develop a new inner world."*

- Dalai Lama

The following 7 steps offers a process to support you in healing and transforming from the past, as a way to experience greater wellness and create more transcendent relationships in the present.

1) **Connect with your Authentic Self**
   Create the space to go inward, to find the peace and security within your own inner connection. This may begin as a meditation practice. Or some will find this space out in nature. But you will want isolation apart from outer distraction and your normal hectic life. You should experience relative mental calmness, and openness for higher guidance.

2) **Clearly state your intentions**
   In this instance you are working within your highest capacity to understand the true value and purpose of specific past relationship experiences. Primarily, the ones in which you still feel stuck, negative, or

disempowered in some way. Your purpose for this exercise is to gain the wisdom that leads to your healing and the release of any energy that is negatively affecting you now. Ask for this guidance, to whatever Source, and in whatever words feel appropriate for you. Give thanks and expressions of gratitude in advance, for this healing process and the higher guidance that is with you now.

3) **Identify the energy blockage or deficit**

You may have a clear image of a specific relationship that continues to feel damaging and disempowering. Remember that you are healing your energy, and not the past relationship. This relationship is in the past, and therefore, no longer exists. The energy, however, may still be kept alive in your mind. Even if you associate your problems with a specific person, this is not about them; it is an energy issue for you.

You attracted this other person as a teacher. Notice how I use the word "teacher" which has a more neutral connotation. To gain the proper perspective you must begin to see this experience more objectively. Referring to them as demon, evil person, asshole, idiot, jerk, etc. will continue to hold you in a victim status. So stop doing this, even in jest.

The situation (whatever it was) did not feel good to your ego, and you were previously unable to absorb the higher lesson designed for your own healing. So you have attached to the pain and disempowerment in the experience. You are now in process of facilitating your own healing – something that you are fully empowered to do. Identify the feelings that come up when you think about this person or that relationship. This is the old energy that you are now transforming into the loving energy that represents your higher truth. If you are having trouble with this, ask for guidance, and be patient.

4) **Focus on your involvement**
Learn to recognize the old negative energies associated with a relationship as the result of your necessity for attracting this experience. Fully accept your responsibility and involvement in the relationship. Your healing involves shifting your awareness to understand that on some level you chose this experience for your ultimate transformation. Your healing is not connected to what they did. That is a separate matter. And what they did in the past is not relevant to you in your own higher space now. **You must accept full accountability for yourself**. Other people are accountable for themselves.

See yourself in the various scenarios in which you have been negatively impacted. Notice how you acted toward, reacted to, allowed, or otherwise participated in the events or situations you are examining. Use your higher awareness to see the truth. But do this from the inner space of self-love. Your healing is a natural process in overcoming previous situations in which you were disconnected from your higher truth. Do not attach to, or continue to discharge, any fearful energy such as guilt, embarrassment, judgment, etc. Within this process you are consciously replacing any arising fear with the energy of self-love.

5) **What have you learned about yourself and the relationship?**
Relating to Step 4, if you were functioning within a more conscious and loving awareness you would have possessed a greater inner strength, self-image, and understanding of your true higher value. You would

have stood more firmly in your truth, and protected your own energy instead of attaching to theirs. You would not have handed over your power to them. No judgement, just truth.

Now ask yourself the following questions:

1. If I had been empowered in this way at the time, how would I have acted or expressed myself differently?
2. How would this relationship have gone or ended differently?
3. How will I honor myself moving forward? (If this relationship is still ongoing.)
4. Can I now realize and accept that I was given an opportunity to more fully honor and value myself?
5. Can I now accept that this may have been my higher purpose for attracting this person?
6. Can I now accept that I am in control of my choices when connected to my higher truth in the present moment?

Deeply consider the answers to those questions.

6) Release the teacher with love
Because of your relationship with this teacher you have been given an opportunity to heal, grow, and evolve in higher wisdom. This may bring benefit to you on both a human and spiritual level. You are not condoning or approving of the thoughts, words, and actions made by another that may have come from their fear and ego-delusion. Yet you can now accept that what was done is done. With renewed energy and understanding you may now make choices that are more empowering. So release this teacher with sincere gratitude for their role in your ascension.

There are two main reasons why you now want to offer only loving thoughts for this person going forward. One, you are grateful for the benefit received that has led you to greater self-love, self-awareness, and accountability for your life and wellness. And two, at their core they are Spirit just as you are, yet they may have been disconnected from their truth and unaware of their own love and empowerment. So be compassionate toward all others.

Note: this does not make them your problem to fix! Simply release them in love.

7) **Offer gratitude to Spirit**
Always express appreciation for the blessings you receive. Spirit works tirelessly and unconditionally on your behalf all of the time. In this instance you have intentionally connected with higher guidance for your purpose in healing some negative energy that has disturbed your peace and wellness.

You may now reside in a lighter, more loving energetic state as you create more transcending relationships. Additionally, the energy of gratitude is immensely supportive toward shifting your perception of reality. This allows you to appreciate what is, instead of following the ego tendency to focus more on what you don't have.

Utilize this process as needed to help you heal and release any disempowering energies. You may also want to add some affirmations to reinforce your empowerment, or help you to manifest your new higher desires. For a clearer, healthier, truer perspective of your life and experiences, connect with your inner truth as often as possible.

CHAPTER 17

Service Is a Higher Purpose

*"If we have no peace, it is because we have forgotten
that we belong to each other."*

- Mother Theresa

As we are given the opportunity to learn, heal, grow, and transform from our relationships, we are serving the higher purpose of our own evolution. Another higher purpose for relationships is to serve others. This is the recognition that all beings are worthy within their true higher nature, and that our life paths are interrelated.

It is always best to serve others within our higher consciousness. In this way we are coming from a more unconditionally-loving energetic space. Therefore, we are not attaching to the negative energies that may later necessitate a need for healing. We may then intentionally create more relationships that are based in truth and that reinforce our loving energy while being mutually beneficial.

We have created our past relationships through a common attraction of our energy. Whether this was primarily based in Spirit or ego will manifest in the quality of the exchange between us. However, you may now notice past relationships that brought with them situations or circumstances in which you were required to be of service to someone else. In other words, there was an additional purpose, beyond the consequences leading to your opportunity to heal.

Maybe this was pertinent to you as a part of your upbringing. For instance, a family member was disabled or had limited capacity in some way, and needed additional help from you. This likely was an obligation accepted within your Soul group connection prior to your birth. On an ego level you may have considered this an imposition or hindrance to your happiness. And based on that perception you might have accumulated negative energy that has been disempowering to you. In truth it was part of the life path designed by your Spirit, and therefore, on that level, you are benefitting.

If you continue to have negative energy around this situation, you may need to consider your role in service as a higher commitment. Accept this as a part of fulfilling your Soul's purpose, and not merely a detriment to some worldly attainment. In truth, these experiences are offering you the opportunity that you need for your evolution. Also, endeavor to place more of your awareness upon the higher value that your assistance offers this person on a human level – you are supporting them in fulfilling their purpose as well.

Another situation where service seems to be placed upon our path will come from adult relationships. Let's say that you engaged in a very challenging relationship for a period of time that proved to be a temporary connection. And maybe you were put in a position to be obligated to serve or support their children or someone close to them.

You have been given an opportunity to serve on a higher level. This goes beyond the attraction and lessons involved with the primary person you are relating to. When the relationship ends, these other souls you were serving will be removed from your life. Depending upon your role and connection with them, this may be difficult. However, work to release your attachment to them, knowing that this was your role for a specific period of time. You have now fulfilled your obligation in their service.

I believe that we attract our relationships for many reasons that may serve our spiritual journey. And sometimes the only way these temporary connections make sense is to accept that their Souls needed our help for the time we were together. This may include losing a child, either through death or divorce. If you continue to grieve over a loss or ending, try to elevate your perception of the situation. Once their time with you has concluded then their path has taken them in a new direction. And regardless of how our ego perceives this, it is always for their higher benefit.

For the sake of your wellness, and the fulfillment of your remaining journey, you must learn to be at peace with this truth. I have personally had this experience in my life. So I understand both the human and spiritual dimension involved. It may take some time and practice, but the truth will set you free.

Additionally, we are called to offer service in our primary relationships. I have spent some time talking about how we attract "teachers" in the form of relationship partners, so that we may learn our truth. In this way they are serving us. Well, the reverse is true as well. They have attracted us into their life to teach them what they need to learn about themselves.

Just as is the case for all teachers, we have no control over whether or not the "student" will learn the lesson. In truth, this is not our job. The job of the teacher is to simply offer the lesson or message and allow the student to fulfill their destiny. It is never within our control to fix or heal anyone else.

So within the context of your healing from a past relationship, as a part of your higher understanding of its purpose, you were called to serve them on a Soul level. As we know, this may not have felt good at all from your human/ego perspective. Regardless, spiritual law always brings what we need.

Our best path for healing is to acknowledge and accept the higher truth of our past experiences. From a place connected to our Authentic Self, we function within a more unconditionally loving energy. Find the enthusiasm for this idea of service, and this may add another layer of spiritual truth that helps you to release the past with love.

PART II: Exercises

1) Examine certain significant conditions, circumstances, or conflicts within your childhood relationships. What are your current feelings about your past experiences or the people involved? How has this impacted your view of your life as an adult? Upon examination, can you understand where you now need to honor and find value in these experiential lessons designed to teach you to live your own truth?

2) Examine certain significant intimate relationships from your past. From the perspective of full accountability (higher truth), look at the events and experiences that you attracted and created. Can you see where you could have made more empowering choices had you been able to realize greater self-love and value? Would you still have engaged in this relationship? If so, how would you have handled it differently for more success and wellness? If not, how would you choose differently now, within a new higher perspective?

3) For any relationship from the past that continues to bring fearful thoughts or otherwise be an energy drain, complete the *7 Steps for Healing and Transformation*. Afterwards, are you able to notice a greater inner peace and wellness? Do you feel lighter and more empowered? This healing may occur incrementally, so continue this process until you are fully able to release the fear and claim your power.

PART II: Affirmations

I AM now realizing the greater lessons of my past relationships

I AM now accountable for all that I create and attract in my life.

I AM now empowered to heal and grow from my past.

I AM now grateful for all of the teachers in my life.

I AM now forgiving of myself and all others.

I AM now grateful for the past that has led to greater self-love.

I AM now empowered and unattached to the energy of others.

I AM now responsible for my own wellness and wholeness.

I AM now grateful for my path of growth and transcendence.

I AM now grateful for the relationships that have taught me to love and honor myself.

I AM now living my greatest value and purpose.

PART III:

OFFER YOUR LOVING PRESENCE TO OTHERS

"When you take your attention into the present moment, a certain alertness arises. You become more conscious of what's around you, but also, strangely, a sense of presence that is both within and without."

- Eckhart Tolle

PART III: Prologue

The quality of our current relationships is dependent upon the extent to which we are able to honor and live our higher truth (Part I). This is to be supported by the inner healing and growth from releasing the false and disempowering energy that we attached to from past relationships (Part II). How do we value ourselves? What is it that we need/desire to experience at this point in our lives? Who are we attracting to further facilitate and support our healing and growth process? The answers to these questions will be revealed in our current and future relationships.

Regardless of our relationship status we are obligated to fulfill our true higher purpose within this human experience. There is great potential for both spiritual and human fulfillment within all of our relationships (not just our intimate partnerships). It is just a matter of living within a connection to our Authentic Self, and honoring our truth. Therefore, as we develop our greatest inner power and awareness, we will interact with others in a more kind, considerate, supportive, and compassionate way. We are now ready to receive great benefit in offering our loving presence in all of our relationships.

As we are more conscious of the energy exchanged in each present moment, we will become aware of the impact we have on others, as well as their impact upon us. From this elevated state of awareness we will be empowered to choose love over fear in all interpersonal situations. By doing so, we enhance the opportunity to maintain our wellness, while honoring others. Ultimately this leads to transcending relationships and the higher quality of Unity Consciousness.

PART III: Energetic Quality or Tool

Within the principle of offering your loving presence to all others, is the energetic quality of **UNCONDITIONAL LOVE**. This may sound obvious, but it's not so simple. This represents the manifestation of your awakening and inner spiritual practice. It is the highest of Divine qualities, and therefore the highest expression in which you may share with others.

Your expression of energy to all people represents your true inner state of Divine connection. Your ability to offer the energy of Unconditional Love is based upon your level of self-love and higher consciousness. This is the culmination of realizing your Authentic Self, and claiming the power of each present moment – the keys to Self-Mastery. This takes great inner strength and a higher understanding of the value of all lives, also known as Unity Consciousness.

The opposite energetic quality therefore is **FEAR**. This represents the absence of Unconditional Love. Until we have sufficiently focused on our own healing and growth, people most often reside within this disconnected space. This is something that all of humanity still must work on, and is always ongoing. Fear is the original source of anger, sadness, grief, greed, insecurity, vanity, jealousy, judgement, intolerance, and indifference. You may notice that these lower qualities have been routinely associated with our human nature, and therefore our relations. Yet, this is a lower state of being.

Therefore, while intentionally creating transcending relationships of all kinds, we must elevate our consciousness through our personal healing and growth. As was discussed in Part I, this is the primary value of our relationships on a spiritual level. From there we may express more Unconditional Love to others in support of their journey as well as ours.

CHAPTER 18
Express Thy Self

"Your personality is here to serve the energy of your soul."

- Oprah Winfrey

In Part I, I talked about knowing thyself. So now with a greater knowledge of your path and purpose, along with the releasing of the negative energy accumulated from past relationship experiences, you may be ready to express your higher truth into the world. This will form the basis of the creation of new, more transcendent relationships.

Expressing your loving energy or presence to all others is the outer expansion of the love within you. When you are not experiencing this inner love then you will not express loving energy. Of course, for better or worse, we have always expressed our self in some form or fashion. Our goal is to now express ourselves in the ways that create what it is that we wish to experience within our relationships. When we may have previously resided in so much fear and delusion, we encountered experiences that were unsupportive to our wellness and happiness. While valuable as a teaching tool to help us re-align with our higher love and truth, they were nonetheless unsatisfying from our human perspective.

As we have learned that we are fully accountable for our choices, and it is within our power to choose love over fear, we have a whole new potential for empowerment. The application of this power will be developed through the ongoing practice of shifting our thoughts and self-talk to recognize and realize our truth as we continue to create our new reality. This is based in the realization of our true identity – our Authentic Self.

Next, we must utilize our awareness within the present moment. This higher awareness allows us to recognize our presence in love, or our disconnection in fear. This is critical to the quality of our energetic expressions. In this moment we are conscious. We notice ourselves from a higher perspective. If we momentarily lose this consciousness, it is our awareness that will lead us to reconnect to our truth.

Another key factor in this "transformation" is that we are now learning to trust and honor our truth. We have never been fully disconnected from our truth, wisdom, or inspiration. It is just that as humans (egos) we often have either been too distracted to hear it, or too fearful to accept it. We all have had some horrific experiences that never would have manifested had we been loving/strong enough to trust our own instincts and truth.

A primary purpose for teaching people to embrace their enlightened path is to get them to become aware of the true power that lives within them. In this world people are so focused on instantaneous ego gratification, the easy path of following others, and on maintaining a hectic stressful pace. In order to claim your true path and purpose, you must be able to create the space to go within, to hear the wisdom that is speaking directly to you. As you become aware of this gift, you then must choose to love and honor yourself enough to heed this special wisdom.

Now you have greater power to create a reality that utilizes your unique gifts, qualities, interests, and passion. These things represent your higher, inner self, and they are different for each of us. The longer you seek the world's ambition, systems, methods, and delusion, over your own truth, the more disconnected and disempowered you will feel. The goal is not to avoid this world, but to integrate your truth (Spirit) within it.

Within your highest presence you will honor your truth. Therefore, when it comes to relationships and interacting with others, you will honor your own wellness. Eventually, through practice, you will come to know this as your reality. This empowerment is directed from within, which means that you no longer need to take energy from other people in order to sustain yourself. This is a huge shift!

Expressing loving energy is synonymous with offering your loving presence. Having come from a previous position of being controlled by ego, this is a process that may develop incrementally. Be patient with yourself. A lifetime of fear is a challenging thing to overcome. And the voice that says, "You can't do this, you're not (good enough, strong enough, worthy enough, loving enough, healthy enough, etc.)," is simply a reminder of the fearful energy that remains within. Patience is a quality of love that will be required often, regarding you and other people. But as you develop your self-love, and then offer your loving expressions more often, this inner/outer energy will shift to be more supportive.

A great deal of this is intention and practice, i.e. *Mindfulness* and *Accountability*. It is available to all people. However, if transforming your life is not a priority, then you will continue along the same path you always have. This life you are living is significant, it is what you have chosen as your human experience. Therefore, it seems reasonable to live it within your highest potential for wellness and fulfillment. This will have the greatest impact upon your relationship with others and your influence in the world.

CHAPTER 19

Accept Others as They Are

*"Acceptance looks like a passive state, but in reality it brings
something entirely new into this world. That peace,
a subtle energy vibration, is consciousness."*

- Eckhart Tolle

Expressing your loving energy or presence to all others is the outer expansion of the love within you. The acceptance of others, on the other hand, is the allowing for the existence of their energetic state. This acceptance is based in the Divine spiritual qualities of awareness, compassion, and self-love. It is essential for creating transcending relationships.

In reality, you can hate, ignore, or disapprove of the energy expressions of others, yet that does not stop it from being their truth in the moment. This reflects the inner energy they are experiencing at the time. Maybe this is their typical state of being, or maybe they are presently dealing with something extraordinary for them. The value of their experience is not for us to judge, it is only for us to accept.

Yet, how we allow it to impact us is a different matter. Within our inner power and truth we can choose how best to react or reply. We can notice how our energy is affected and then choose to remain connected to love. This means that we are honoring ourselves and accepting them in this moment.

This is an enlightened way of being with the people in whom you associate on a regular basis, as well as for interactions with relative strangers. The point for us is not to get caught up in their delusion. This is not to say that they are "right or wrong," but to determine if their expressions are truth for us. Our purpose is to choose to remain connected to our own empowerment.

In addition to not attaching our energy to their delusion, it is not for us to decide what the truth is for someone else. They are expressing their truth as they see it, based upon a myriad of factors that are relevant only to them. So from that standpoint, who are we to say they are wrong. They may likely have a different perspective than us, yet we each may hold to our truth without the other being controlled, judged, corrected, or reprimanded. It is not our job, nor is it within our true capability to "fix" or change anyone else.

We have a choice to accept others as they are, while still honoring our inner love and truth. Oftentimes the "meaning" of what we perceive from others is conjured up in our own minds and prejudices anyway. Remember, we have our own countless factors that determine our perceptions. In addition to that, often our communication skills are quite deficient.

While connected to your highest truth there is nothing that anyone can say to you that can directly cause you to be angry, hurt, disappointed, etc. These are always choices we make, and are tied to our fear and expectations. Therefore, we will easily attach a negative meaning to most anything that other people say to or about us that connects to our fear. I hope that you can see that this is a real problem which we all deal with.

While we are always in process of healing, growth, and evolution, we are sometimes connected to love and at other times attached to fear. The whole point of "spiritual" practice is to reside within our loving place that is connected to our Spirit as often as possible. You absolutely have the potential to achieve a greater state of enlightened living. And you certainly will have plenty of opportunities to "practice," or interact with relatively unconscious people.

So accepting others is a way of allowing them to be who they are, and this need not force any form of negativity upon us.

From here, depending upon the purpose of the relationship, we can decide if it is generally supportive to our well-being, or generally unsupportive. And then we may choose to modify, continue, or discontinue the relationship. From the place of your higher identity, you are always authorized to choose to honor your truth and support your own wellness.

While we are to accept others as they are, we are never to ignore our wellness or dishonor our truth. We may find a higher meaning and value in a relationship and consciously choose, from a place of love, to stay connected with this person. Or if they are on any level harmful and offer no real higher value, then we are often best served to release them and move on. If for some reason, someone else decides to move on from us, we must release our attachment to them and accept this as well.

When we are dishonoring ourselves we will put the impetus of the decision making about our wellness upon other people. This is a position of fear, not self-love. We may ask them to change in order to continue the relationship. Or we may continue to stay until they finally do something that we can no longer tolerate, even though they have shown us all along who they are.

Here is an example of dishonoring and deferring your own power. Maybe you have witnessed people at work who constantly complain about their job, boss, working conditions, etc. Yet they will never choose to leave, until they are fired. This is because their outer energetic expressions represent their inner fearful nature. Deep down they don't think they deserve better. So, while they are unhappy, at the same time they feel powerless. All of this will negatively affect their life on many levels. Interestingly enough, if they do get fired they will typically express disappointment and anger at that. This is because they were so attached to their victim energy, and while quite unsatisfying, they have grown comfortable with this identity. Now they must shift to be more accountable for their wellness, or otherwise create further lessons in suffering.

You must be able to accept what is, and not simply wish for it to be otherwise. When we are accountable for our own well-being we will notice with awareness that our job no longer supports our interest, passion, or purpose. Then we will begin to formulate plans to find a job that honors our higher truth. We always have choices. And even if something happens completely outside of our awareness, we can choose to accept it as our reality, and shift to higher ground.

You likely will notice the same self-sabotage or choice to honor ourselves within our intimate relationships. How often do people complain about their partner? Even if they say they are just "venting," they are expressing negative energy that in some way is controlling them within. If you want to move toward greater wellness and empowerment in this type of relationship you have a choice. You can honestly communicate with your partner by expressing your truth in a loving way, and by fully hearing their truth. Or you can continue to live within this negativity which is blocking your full empowerment and happiness.

On the enlightened path, what you can't do is dishonor your truth, or not accept their truth. The quality of our outer circumstances does not change without addressing our inner energetic expressions and needs. And what shows up outside reveals your inner state of wellness. Certainly, you can still choose to stay in a relationship or job without healing anything, or experiencing the love, peace, and joy that you deserve. Do I need to say it again – we always have choices.

So in all of your circumstances you must accept the truth of a situation or other person involved. Do not live under the delusion and disempowerment that things should be different or other than they really are. Accountability dictates that you work with what is, and address the real truth for purposes of your own healing, growth, and ascension. Now you are empowered to create greater wellness and transcendent relationships.

CHAPTER 20

Marriage – A Sharing of Journeys

"Coming together is a beginning; keeping together is progress; working together is success."

- Henry Ford

Marriage is probably the most encompassing of all adult relationships. It requires our greatest exertion of energy, and is the commingling of all aspects of our life. Additionally, it is a contractual agreement, which brings the legal system into play. It represents a significant commitment between two people who are (ideally) planning to share their lives together. This may bring certain societal and practical advantages, and for some people there is a moral or religious feature.

Spiritually speaking, this is a relationship that offers a significant potential for the sharing of your Soul journey within the human experience. Every day you have countless interactions in which you engage each other with the expression of your inner energy. Therefore, you will have an unparalleled opportunity to work out your healing, growth, and ascension with this other human/Soul partner.

From the human standpoint you will co-create your lifestyle. This includes intimacy, home space, careers, hobbies, finances, possibly children and in-laws, maybe ex-spouses, and likely even your circle of friends. This is quite a tall order, especially when this is supposed to last the balance of your lifetime. If over 50% of marriages end in divorce it is certainly understandable. So as they say, "What's love got to do with it?"

Your intention is to build this loving, happy, and fulfilling life together. You are each an individual and at the same time a unit of two. This is a very challenging combination of experiencing life together in each present moment, combined with numerous long-term expectations. As an overall endeavor, this would seem to require a tremendous amount of faith. On top of this, in order to truly be empowered you each must have sufficient autonomy for the sake of growth, evolution, and the fulfillment of your own unique purpose.

A great many factors go into the equation of a successful and satisfying marriage. It starts not only with whom you have chosen for a partner, but of course, your own energetic state of wellness that attracted this person. The key issues involved deal with the quality of your own inner love and connection to your higher truth. How much do you love yourself? How well do you know yourself? How well are you expressing your truth? This will determine whether you chose a partner primarily from love or fear, and from wisdom or ignorance.

Regardless of how you came together, if you are willing to awaken in the present, you may create the opportunity to share your loving presence together. And you may jointly support the healing, growth, and empowerment of each of you individually and as a couple. This requires higher intention or consciousness in order to shift the focus from ego to Spirit. The truth and energy of this wisdom is valid, whether or not you would ever use this terminology.

If you are living within your highest truth and wellness at the time you attract your partner, you will have the greatest opportunity to connect on that level from the beginning. You may find greater compatibility, not only on the issues that are most supportive to sharing a life together, but also in the ways you express your energy for love instead of fear. If you are presently single, but hope to marry one day, this is of course the best path. Since I have covered in great detail the importance of inner healing leading to a more positive outer attraction, I will focus this chapter on those who are already married.

By the way, for purposes of this teaching, when I use the term marriage, I am including other significant committed long-term relationships as well. You may have opted not to make it legal. However the same "sharing of journeys" principles apply. You will still be required to offer your loving presence to your partner on a daily basis.

So, you are currently married. I hope that you are finding this to be satisfying and fulfilling to your Spirit and your humanity! Whether you know it or not, you have chosen to support your own healing and growth while connected to your mate. Fulfilling your own Soul's purpose is the most important thing, and the reason you have chosen this human experience. Whether you choose to honor this truth or not, it will always be your primary obligation. This is the highest reality for both you and your spouse. So for the sake of your higher fulfillment, leading to greater satisfaction as a couple, it is critical that you each grow to honor yourselves and the other in this way.

You are sharing your journeys together. On the level of Spirit, you are not ending your individual journey, and starting a new joint journey. In this way, marriage is a human endeavor, not a spiritual one. It can still be treated as sacred, but it does not override your accountability for your own higher journey and path.

However, beyond your accountability to your own truth, the commitment to your partner is real and meaningful. It's just that it should not supersede your own truth and wellness. Not just for your sake, but for the marriage as well. For if you are unable to function within a connection to loving energy, due to an over-abundance of fearful energy created in the partnership, you will be unable to honor yourself or your marriage.

Here is what love has to do with it. We must be able to love ourselves before we can love others. Our inner love must be strong enough to heal and shift us from our own self-destructive beliefs and behaviors. Beyond that, we must be able to claim our power in the present moment regarding our interactions together in order to offer this love to our partner (and others). If the combined energies of the two partners are as negative and toxic as to prohibit you from sufficiently experiencing and expressing the energy of love, you cannot be fulfilled or satisfied together.

This is just spiritual law. You may find some temporary consolation in certain human achievements or conditions. But more than likely these will be temporary and quite insufficient. If you are finding great challenges sharing your loving energy space together, then you need to each be fully accountable for understanding the true causes of these difficulties.

We could detail any number of possible problems from our human perspective. However, all of these potentialities boil down to two things. One, are you willing to be accountable for honoring your higher truth and expressing your loving presence? And two, are you willing to accept your partner as they are, while they are embarking on their own awakening process? When you are each doing this, you will be sharing your personally journey in a mutually supportive manner.

This is the truth for all relationships, not just marriage. However, being married offers the greatest of tests because of the constant nature of the interactions; and because of this, you will each encounter the full range of highs and lows within yourself and coming from the other. Our human experience may throw so many challenges at us that this can (and often does) distract us from our higher truth, and deflect our true power. We get caught up in all of the worldly activities that draw out our egos and exhaust our energy, and then before we know it, we are bickering with our loving partner.

Early recognition of our inner energetic deficit will prevent a multitude of external suffering. Whenever we notice our energy moving in that direction we should recognize the need to shift our focus within. We may locate the origin of negativity that is now manifesting as a "problem." From here we can exercise our higher consciousness to find solutions based in love and support. This is how we consistently elevate the quality of the marriage and our life in general.

So, if you are generally functioning together in a healthy, supportive manner (regardless of outside circumstances), you are fulfilling your purpose together. However, if you are creating great tension and suffering (again, independent of outside circumstances), then you are likely blocking your loving energy. And your Spirit is showing you the need for healing and shifting in some form.

This does not necessarily mean that staying married is hopeless. What is needed (always) is to be fully accountable to yourself and your spouse in working through the process of inner healing and growth. You do not each have to be at the same place in this process. After all, you are each on your own unique path, and part of your purpose together is to support and encourage your partner to experience their best energy. However, you are severely handicapped if one person is completely unconscious and is unwilling to pursue their own wellness, or if your partner is not willing to accept your truth.

If your marriage is dysfunctional and disempowering to this degree, then seek the help you need and consider moving on. You are here in this life for a higher purpose than simply to stay together. You have no right to control your spouse, nor do they have the right to control you. As difficult and painful as divorce can be, this is the natural human consequence of selecting a life mate while relatively unconscious. I know, because I have done this.

Divorce is the inherent risk of choosing a marriage partner unwisely, or in falsely believing that this was to be a lifelong connection. There is no condemnation in that statement, it is simply the truth. So if necessary, have the courage to honor yourself and your spouse, and heal, grow and experience your highest life apart from each other.

Now, having gone there, my sincere hope is that you and your spouse are willing to learn from the outer experiences that are showing up as unsatisfying or unfulfilling. And that you will then sincerely tune in to the energetic qualities that are the cause. Of course, satisfaction and fulfillment are internal qualities and, therefore, must be developed and practiced by each of you within yourselves. However, our partner will have great influence as to how challenged or successful we are in this process.

If there is sufficient love energy within the relationship, then work together to support each other in the development and creation of a more connected life. Accountability, acceptance, and honest communication are key elements toward healing and growing as individuals and as a couple. When you are able to approach your inner wellness with the attention and intention required, you will be able to create outer conditions that honor your love and lifestyle together.

CHAPTER 21

Single Can Be Healthy and Empowering

"To conquer oneself is the best and noblest victory; to be vanquished by one's own nature is the worst and most ignoble defeat."

-Plato

Now let's talk about being single in the healthiest way. So why is "single" being written about in a book called ***Transcending Relationships***? First, there are far more transcendent relationships to experience than simply the one that includes a spouse. Second, more and more people are living this "status" called single, so the inner wellness of those involved is critically important. And finally, the greatest relationship we may experience involves the integration of our Spirit into our humanity, this is how we co-create our lives with the Divine.

One who learns to awaken to their greatest inner love and wellness is well positioned to create the most successful and empowering relationships of all types.

Being single offers a wonderful opportunity to prioritize this inner journey of healing, growth, and transcendence. Recent statistics show that for the first time in the United States there are more single than married adults. Therefore, wouldn't it be catastrophic to have so many people live disempowered within a mindset and belief that says that we must be married (or similarly connected to one life partner) in order to be happy? It is not only disempowering, it is false. Marriage is a lifestyle preference, while happiness and fulfillment are internal qualities of wellness.

Regarding your level of wellness as a single person, there are some important questions you should answer for yourself. What feelings come up when you think about being single? Do you think of this as a choice, or an undesired condition or status? Are you utilizing this experience to create a balanced, empowered, and fulfilling life? If not, then why not? Are you struggling and wishing for a partner? If yes, then why? The answer to these questions will say a lot about your current level of energetic wellness. It will also tell me about what you are likely creating in your future.

Whether single or married, we are accountable for our unique life path and wellness. A great falsehood is that "once I am married I no longer am fully responsible for myself." This will ensure an unsatisfactory and unfulfilling life, and likely a co-dependent relationship.

Our greatest human purpose is to develop our life to be the expression of our love, joy, peace, holistic wellness, contribution, and fulfillment. These are all Divine inner qualities. So the integration of this into our humanity is a very worthwhile human achievement. Once you begin to approach this quality of enlightened living, you may notice great self-sufficiency, satisfaction, and higher fulfillment in experiencing your life. Of course, all of this may be achieved while you are single.

So with regard to entering a formal, committed long-term relationship, you would only be interested in this when choosing a partner who **ADDS** to the already wonderful, healthy life you have created within yourself. To partner with anyone for any other reason would be unwise, and the cause to manifest additional lessons around relationships. Be accountable for your own wellness, and then with your higher energy and motivations choose your path. To feel the "need" for a partner is not your highest energy.

In truth, our desire for one form of lifestyle over another is based on the perception of "the grass is always greener ..." syndrome. I'm not happy here, so maybe I will be happy over there. You do not ever escape your own inner energetic space or need for healing. Develop yourself into a loving force, and then notice how green your grass is in any circumstance.

This is the great opportunity to establish and fortify one's inner health and empowerment while single. You may more easily be responsible for your thoughts, words, feelings, and actions, without the constant interaction and opinion from a partner. You can take the time, if you have not already done so, to really know yourself. To do this as an adult, without undue influence from anyone as close as a spouse, can be powerful.

What are your unique gifts, skills, interests, passions, and purpose? Are you now able to combine higher understanding with great freedom and flexibility to create and manifest your dreams? Even if one of your dreams is to have the ideal life partner, this is only one dream out of many. Plus, your ability to connect to your truth, and reinforce your love energy, passion, and purpose is highly supportive toward attracting your best mate.

What do you want to do professionally? What is your purpose and highest contribution in service to the world? What have you always wanted to learn or experience? What hobbies sound like fun? What can you tick off of your bucket list? Are you creating empowering relationships with friends and family? What healthy habits may you commit to for the sake of holistic wellness? What is your desire for dating?

"But I'll have to clean, cook, and do laundry for myself." So what? "I may have to hire a handyman to do or fix things." Again, so what? "I may have to live with less stuff, with one income instead of two." This may be true, but you can also control your expenses much better. And besides, most of us accumulate more stuff than we really need. Better to experience your best fulfillment and satisfaction within, than to merely collect a bunch of non-essential possessions without. Your things will not bring you true and lasting happiness.

"Yes, but I will have to spend time alone." Ah ha! That's the real challenge for most people. It seems to be literally painful for some people to face their own truth, and find satisfaction in their own space. Our thoughts say, "What would I be without another person to make me feel whole and valued?" The truth of your essence does not change either way, you are always a spiritual being having a human experience. It is always up to us to find how this life path is valuable and purposeful.

Some may think that they will get lost in their silence. Yet maybe you would finally hear your inner voice of truth and know that you are ENOUGH. "What would I do, and how could I survive on my own?" You came into this world alone, and you will leave it alone as well. You might learn how special and gifted you truly are if you ever gained the confidence and courage to find out.

Single can involve dating often, occasionally, or not at all. This will depend upon your desire for physical intimacy in relation to other goals. If you want to have sex, go ahead – safely. However, I would not advise forming a relationship (or getting married) for the sake of having sex regularly. Sex is no consolation for a bad relationship, and you are obligating yourself to a great many things, just to have that sex.

Find your best companionship with people you like to spend time with. Develop the kind of empowering relationships you desire with your friends and family. I believe that being single requires a much greater proactive approach to living your life. You may discover virtually unlimited opportunities, but you must be willing to create the experiences that are most fulfilling. When with a partner it is easy to fall back and let someone else dictate what is "good" for you. There is certainly an element of settling.

I realize that this may sound like more work than some people want. It is human nature to let others decide our lifestyle for us. Yet, a truly empowering marriage or partnership can be extremely rewarding. My point is not to talk anyone out of wanting to be married. However, while you are single, whether this is just temporary or it's your long-term choice, it can be incredibly fulfilling and empowering.

Always decide what is best for you. But do this from a place of power and higher love, and not the delusion of fear. No one else, not family, society, or me can tell you what is right for you. Be empowered within your own truth, and then express this in all ways within your chosen life path.

Being single can be an optimal time to connect with your Authentic Self. While it is true that you are responsible for fulfilling all of your human needs without a partner's assistance, you can extend this level of accountability to your spiritual practice as well. The other side of that coin is that unless you do find sufficient focus on the spiritual self, you will likely waste this valuable time in pursuit of distractions, addictions, and ego gratification.

Find the joy in committing to yourself. Don't be single because you think no one wants you. *Single is a choice!* So choose to become the highest version of yourself. If that should lead to a relationship, then it is likely to be a satisfying one; and if it doesn't then you have learned to love and honor yourself, without requiring another person to make you feel better about your life. You may find that you are able to offer great service to the world, unencumbered by a life partner. Always choose to honor your truth, on the enlightened path.

CHAPTER 22

What about Friendships?

"The glory of friendship is not the outstretched hand, not the kindly smile, nor the joy of companionship; it is the spiritual inspiration that comes to one when you discover that someone else believes in you and is willing to trust you with a friendship."

- Ralph Waldo Emerson

Beyond our family, and our intimate relationships, we will connect with certain people throughout our lives in whom we may choose to share our space and energy in a more casual way. We call these friends. Sometimes we may have friendly relations with our co-workers, yet our purpose together centers around our jobs. The friends that I am focusing on are the people we spend time with simply for enjoyment.

Yet, what does this actually mean, and is this the real reason we are with these people? Every relationship involves an energetic connection. We attract people for purposes that relate to our energetic expressions and need for healing, growth, and ascension. And this is just as true for our friendships.

A friend may be comforting in our time of need, or inspiring in their support of our dreams. While we walk this journey alone, and alone are responsible for our lives, friendships may be utilized to connect us to our truth. We can at times get lost in the deception of our own mind, but in our associations we may find a new perception and appreciation of all that we are here to be. There is of course a healthy balance to be found between solitude and companionship, and it is here that our friendships may be most valuable.

Depending upon our intimate relationship status, and the desires of our personality, we may endeavor to have many friends, or are quite satisfied with only a few. The length and intensity of these relationships speak to the ongoing nature and quality of the connection. Therefore, we may have friendships that serve their purpose in a relatively short time span; while we may remain connected with other friends for many years. Just as we are each individual Souls having a human experience, the same is true for our friends. Our purpose and needs are different than theirs, and yet, for a period of time there is a mutual exchange of energy and value.

Depending upon our level of inner wellness, we may join with people who either support our healing and growth, or who otherwise diminish our light and pull away our energy. According to this realization of our experience together, when sufficiently awakened, we may choose to continue to expand our light together, or we may decide to terminate the connection. With our intentions toward enlightenment, transcending relationships are always ultimately mutually supportive.

As we continue to evolve, connected to our Authentic Self, we will evaluate our current relationships. You may want to consider a series of questions. Is this still a beneficial association, or have we exhausted any positive purpose for maintaining this friendship? Do we still share common interests and goals? Do we have fun together, or is it too intense, negative, or confrontational?

An important factor here is that you are choosing love. Through your higher identity you love yourself enough to create the conditions that are most supportive to your well-being. Additionally, you are either releasing or remaining connected to a friend from the position of love and compassion. Within this inner healthy space we don't blame or harbor resentment or anger when a relationship ends. It is not anyone's fault. It simply has served its purpose, and is now complete.

If this was an ending that seemed to come from the other person, we have an opportunity to understand and work with the energy that comes up for us. This may feel like sadness, confusion, self-pity, or anger – all different masks of FEAR. It is likely that this other person recognized that an ending was appropriate for them before we accepted this truth for ourselves. And it is just as likely that we have attached our energy to the ego gratification of labeling them our friend.

Somehow we were unwilling to fully care for ourselves and have become reliant upon this other person to fulfill our own needs. This is always our responsibility and not theirs. Therefore, as you go within for the higher guidance that supports your peace and wisdom, you may resolve this situation and shift your perception from loss to blessing. Reclaim your power for creating and maintaining your own wellness.

Since we are to continually evolve, we can understand that it is natural for many friendships to transform. This transformation may indicate that you are no longer associating with this person, or that the manner and frequency has changed. As you endeavor to be the master of your life, utilize your awareness and higher consciousness to intentionally choose mutually beneficial relationships. Through your spiritual practice in mindfulness, express your loving Presence to all people, in all situations. And therefore, be accountable for the quality of your friendships and those with whom you choose to share your energy and space.

As we awaken and evolve, we will likely choose different friends than before. This may be less about a mental decision, and more about an actual elevation of the energy that we project. This is how enlightened living supports us in all aspects of our life. Since we energetically attract what we need, when we are more aware of our higher identity, what we need is more aligned with our Divine qualities.

Therefore, we previously attracted relationships that brought an opportunity to either elevate our self-love or deal with the consequences of living attached to our lower nature. Maybe we functioned and connected with other people based upon an immature mentality, and now as we evolve, our friendships will change to meet our new energetic state. As we develop we become more conscious of our higher qualities and wellness, and of the resulting challenges from ignoring our truth. So we now more easily honor our path and attract the love, joy, peace, and abundance that support our well-being.

Seek to be a quality friend, and to share a mutually supportive connection. Like any relationship, there is an exchange – a give and take. Venture to reside within your own power, then give and receive from that place. Be as honest and considerate with your friends as you can. You should be able to communicate on a personal level. If this is hindered because you are too afraid to offend, then the energy will stagnate and you will likely lose the healthy attraction.

Our friendships are opportunities to enjoy and share our human experience, offer our loving Presence (in a non-sexual way), and accomplish some aspect of our growth and evolution. However, we must always be conscious of our present moment energy. At times things may be light and fun, and at other times there may be strong disagreements.

As always, it is not simply the external experience or circumstance that determines our wellness. Different people will naturally have different points of view. What is most important is our inner alignment to love and truth. If we determine that this friendship connection feels disempowering and destructive to our inner love and peace, then it is up to us to honor our truth. This is an inner determination, and not a judgement expressed about your friend. Therefore, be mindful of your communication to others and be impeccable with your words. It can never be our intention to harm anyone else, yet our highest obligation is to ourselves.

Our higher purpose is to fully love ourselves, and this is the process that leads to loving all others as well. In this way, a friendship is not a distinction of the people you like versus the ones you don't. Instead, they are the people with whom you choose to hang out and share your personal story. Everyone is simultaneously living their personal human journey, and therefore, no one need be called an enemy. Yet, choose your friendships consciously, as they have the opportunity to more directly impact your energy, wellness, and happiness.

CHAPTER 23

My Experience of Transformation

"When you are inspired by some great purpose, some extraordinary project, all your thoughts break their bounds. Dormant forces, faculties and talents become alive, and you discover yourself to be a greater person by far than you ever dreamed yourself to be."

- Patanjali

In the writing of the *On the Enlightened Path* book series, I intentionally designed the first book to be on the topic of self-mastery, which is supportive of all areas of life. Yet, I instinctively knew that the next book would entail the sharing of higher truth and wisdom into the realm of relationship. This is an area that has been most challenging on my path, and therefore, most supportive to my own transformation.

I am currently in my mid-fifties and have been single for an extended period of time since my last divorce. The full truth for me is I now love my life – as it is. I have learned to love who I AM. And even in the temporary moments of doubt and fear, it is this self-love that is the bridge to the other side. I am not seeking a partner to "make me happy." My ongoing effort and intention is to be responsible for creating my own happiness. I live more in the present, and therefore, maintain openness for what comes next.

For some people, this satisfaction in my own space seems incomprehensible, and to others quite admirable. This depends upon how open or prejudiced their view of what happiness is "supposed" to look like. In other words, people's opinions of us always define them and not us. It has taken me many years to understand this truth, and therefore, I am far less concerned or motivated by what people think of me. I am now learning to live for me while offering my greatest gifts to all; and this has become the basis of my message to others.

I am fully aware that as each of us are here to fulfill our own spiritual journey of evolution and the integration of our Divinity within our humanity, that we all have a different path. No one path is better or greater than another. They are unique. The largest point is to live your path at your highest level of consciousness. My purpose in writing this book is to offer the wisdom made available to me, in support of your total wellness, by utilizing this tool and phenomenon called relationships.

I personally have utilized this tool to encourage a tremendous transformation in my life. I have examined my past experiences to understand my motivation in relationships. I have learned that while not honoring my Authentic Self, I was subjected to those who would take advantage of my gentle nature. I effectively gave away my power in hopes that others would treat me fairly. This lack of accountability was based in fear and insecurity.

I spent years in dysfunctional relationships, thinking that I could "make things work." And then, through divorce and other endings, was required to pick up the pieces and deal with the emotional fallout. Even when I began a relationship thinking that I was "in a good place," my Spirit was giving me an opportunity to trust my instincts and make the empowering choice to not attach to this person, and move in a different direction. So when I ignored the "red flags," and did not honor my truth, I unwittingly chose an experiential lesson in suffering.

Eventually, I chose a relationship partner and experience so bad that I was finally required to awaken to my truth. I endured manipulation, lies, accusations, abuse, and condemnation for my efforts. Needless to say, this ended badly. The blessing was that the marriage was short-lived, yet the healing took much longer. It turns out that the "dark night of the Soul" can last years.

As bad as the marriage was, my recovery may have been more difficult. There was great trauma and loss in this ending, the details of which I prefer not to share. However, beyond the external ramifications, the real work and purpose is internal. I had much confusion, anger, self-doubt, embarrassment, shame, and a sense of hopelessness.

Within my being I knew that this type of relationship could never happen again, and I wasn't even sure that I would survive this time. Why did this happen? What did I do to deserve this? How did I get here? What's wrong with me? How am I ever going to trust again? How will I ever envision a happy future? I learned the worst of what people are capable of in relationship, and it was far beyond anything that I previously thought possible. Clearly, I was quite unprepared for this darkness.

Of course, while your world (or perception of it) is being turned upside down, you are still expected to go to work every day. I was still doing my best to raise my children and be a responsible adult. I tried some counseling for the first time. It felt somewhat satisfying to tell my story of woe to an objective listener. Yet, soon enough, I felt like it just kept me identifying with my tragic experience. The best advice I received was to get back to the gym and exercise, something that has great benefit both psychologically and physically. Additionally, I was guided to a Buddhist nun who began teaching in the area. This was supportive of my higher understanding and inner peace.

Our healing process is a balance of time, intention, and effort. Regardless of the limitations we may see and feel, Spirit is always with us. But sometimes we really have to try hard to find it, because our delusion is great. Our ego feels so victimized. Until we are immersed into the way that the world really works, we believe in this thing called "justice." But that does not really exist in the abstract. When others have an agenda, we cannot rely on them to be fair and impartial. Their motives are not in support of your well-being. Therefore, we must understand that only we are responsible for our welfare.

All of this can lead you to recognize that you are to be the Master of your life. And in order to transform more fully into this realization, you may need to recover from a fall. To awaken, you need to have your ego rocked and your eyes opened. This was true for me. I believe that often the greater our potential for service the greater our transformation must be.

I now know unequivocally that I am responsible for my life and experiences. And all that I create without is first realized within on the level of energy. I attracted a human "teacher" within the context of relationship who taught me a great spiritual truth, regardless of the fact that my humanity was temporarily plunged into darkness and suffering in the process. I have supported my own healing by releasing the negative energy and forgiving all involved. This whole experience was engineered as part of my unique life path, leading to great growth and evolution. Additionally, through this process I was able to receive support from my family that led to a greater connection and appreciation between us.

Regarding relationships, I have learned that none are worth sacrificing yourself for, and that it was always my job to care for my wellness – on all levels. It was my job to define and then honestly communicate my truth within my relationships. While this is not always easy, I now realize that it is essential. I only avoided this responsibility to my detriment.

In the past, I was exposed to higher wisdom, and therefore, intellectually I knew better. Yet, the key is always in the integration of these principles into our humanity. If we want to live enlightened, we first learn and then apply our truth through awareness within each present moment. A great place to start, which was invaluable for me, is maintaining a daily meditation practice. Also, take the steps to shift to healthier habits and relationships.

Our relationships will always mirror back to us our level of energetic wellness, and the integration of our higher truth. Therefore, your inner healing is essential. If that which I have been writing about is not new to you, let it be a reminder to be more diligent toward awakening and shifting your focus now. Be completely honest and courageous. The easy path of denying your truth and relinquishing your power to the will of others will continue to lead to disappointment and suffering. And it is robbing you of valuable time that could otherwise be spent thriving in life and expanding your light.

Within my own sacred space I began to connect with my Authentic Self. My identity that is timeless and connected to higher love. I then chose to honor myself with healthy practices, such as meditation and regular fitness training; activities that are productive to my healing, growth, and ascension. Most importantly I began to create greater awareness to more effectively listen to my inner guidance. I finally committed to listening and trusting. And this awakening was largely spurred by past relationship lessons.

This period of inner focus on wellness, and honoring my higher truth and purpose, has also led me to transition out of a 30 year career. I have shifted my professional service from accountant to author, teacher, and mentor in the areas of personal and spiritual growth and wellness. This has been no small transformation. While my greatest joy and enthusiasm has come within the arena of higher wisdom, I needed to elevate my awareness and the perception of my potential. I was required to face my feelings of vulnerability, and the fear that previously held me back. Understanding my higher identity has supported me in developing the inner strength to be fully accountable for following my dreams.

All of this has enhanced every area of my life, including relationships. I am more present and loving with my children (and now grandchildren), family and friends. Now, should I attract a person who is healthy within her own truth, and who adds to my wonderful life, then I am in the best position to facilitate a loving and transcendent partnership. Yet, this is not my goal or primary focus.

As it comes up within any given present moment, I continue to release the fear that I was holding due to past relationships and false teachings. I have learned to honor my space fully, and to spend my energy with those who are most loving and supportive. I now challenge myself through growth and expansion, and experience the fullness of presence within all of my relationships. In other words I am now beginning to more often live enlightened. As I have stated many times, this is a moment to moment process, so I must endeavor to maintain this connection to my Authentic Self through consistent presence and awareness.

Again, we all have our unique path and challenging lessons from which to transcend. So for whatever constitutes your highest purpose, joy, and fulfillment, you may awaken to your truth and become the master of your life. You have a higher path of service that is needed in the world, which is in alignment with your true gifts, qualities, and passion. You have the potential to express loving energy and thereby attract and maintain healthy, empowered relationships of all kinds. If you have chosen (consciously or not) to be single at this time, my hope is that you will take this opportunity to honor yourself, and take the inner steps to create the amazing life you were meant to live.

CHAPTER 24

Develop Unity Consciousness

"You must be the change you wish to see in the world."

- Mahatma Gandhi

A higher goal within the area of relationships is to develop Unity Consciousness. In my *Mastering Your Life* book (from this series), this is the final of the three keys. First we shift to the higher realization of our truth, next we claim our awareness and power in the present moment, and finally we may cultivate Unity Consciousness which recognizes the higher truth about all others. I hope that you can see how this is eminently valuable toward creating and maintaining transcendent relationships and supporting humankind.

Through much of our life our focus is almost exclusively on ourselves. Our ego is both demanding and fragile, so it takes our constant attention. In some ways this supports us, and in other ways restricts and diminishes us. Yet this is the experience of the unawakened human life.

Next we may develop an awareness of responsibility for certain other humans who are closest to us. This could be our parent's family, our family, friends, and maybe some co-workers. This is advancement from before, yet it may not be far from self-serving. After all, we benefit from these relationships, plus, they can be judged as a reflection of us by other people. We are still overly concerned with our self-image and how we are perceived by others.

The higher state of awakened consciousness is to offer your loving presence to all people. This requires a level of inner healing whereby you are accountable for your own wellness without requiring the energy of others. You are more self-directed in the ways of love and compassion, and this is a form of self-mastery. Our evolution involves honoring ourselves, through self-love, higher awareness, and healthy practices. As we are able to do this, we will have the bandwidth to focus our attention upon others for the sake of THEIR wellness.

Whenever we can reach this level of healing, growth, and ascension, we may offer great benefit to the world. Our loving presence will positively impact those with whom we interact in our lives. Plus, our expressions of loving energy are vibrations that emanate from us as light out into the world. On this level it brings benefit, and counters the high volume of fear that so many others produce. The light always eliminates the darkness and exposes the fear.

In support of your highest evolution, and for the sake of all beings, continue on this enlightened path toward Unity Consciousness. As you fully recognize your Divine light, you will have no choice but to recognize the Divinity in all others as well. This is our higher nature, and not an entitlement for a select few. If you are unable to do this, then this is a reflection of some deeply held beliefs in fear and ego control. Learn to recognize this without judgment or self-loathing, but endeavor to shift toward your higher path and purpose.

Continue to develop your alignment to your highest truth and identity. Learn to love and honor all others, not because they "deserve it" by their behavior, but because this is who you are at your highest level. When you judge another you are actually judging yourself (same for condemning, hating, fearing, trusting, loving, offering compassion, etc.). Better to support and empower yourself and all others, than to be defeated and disempowered within your energy. The world needs all of our light.

CHAPTER 25

The Value of Present Moment Awareness

"Each morning we are born again. What we do today is what matters most."

- Buddha

You now should have an understanding that through your practice in enlightenment you have the ability to be more present, mindful, and aware within all of your interactions and endeavors. This is highly supportive to creating and maintaining empowering relationships. When your focus is in the present moment you may realize a true energetic connection to your life force.

Regarding relationships, you may now ask yourself: Is this interaction/situation supportive or unsupportive? Am I choosing to express love or fear? What is the most appropriate course of action to shift toward love? Am I honoring my truth? Am I honoring and accepting the energy/truth expressed by the other person? Or am I projecting my own thoughts and desires upon them? This level of presence is self-mastery, and supports you on the enlightened path. The goal is to reside in this level of consciousness as often as possible, and to practice to continually improve.

All of this directly supports transcending relationships. When something/someone is pulling or draining your energy, you now may have the where-with-all to determine the best response or action. Sometimes you are required to take a larger more patient view. Your choice for love may be to hold a peaceful space while things develop around you. During this time you are gathering knowledge and sensing your energy. At other times you will remove yourself from a situation or connection that may be harmful or disempowering.

To choose fear would mean that you temporarily lost your present moment connection to higher truth. While disconnected from your Source of love, you will perpetrate and perpetuate any number of negative consequences through your energy that is now controlled by ego. Of course, you would not consciously choose this, so remain aware and present and intentionally create your experiences. This expanded level of mindfulness will lead to your own personal growth and evolution in consciousness.

In addition to being accountable for your own highest wellness, you have an opportunity and obligation to choose love for the benefit of others. By being present you are able to be more aware of how your expressions of energy are impactful to those around you. In addition to honoring your own truth, it is critical to the maintenance of transcending relationships that you honor all others as well. This is called love, consideration, compassion, kindness, etc.

In truth this very thing will create so much more peace, understanding, and acceptance among humans. In the broader sense this supports Unity Consciousness. Yet we may embrace this principle within each and every individual relationship – in each moment. I am sure that you have clearly seen the opposite of this, where people are not concerned about their energetic impact upon others. Obviously this is a very unconscious habit and destructive behavior. We all have a choice in the present moment. How would you like to express your energy to others?

In order to shift to a higher path we must be healthy enough within ourselves, and present enough to claim this power. It must become more of a priority for us to share our light for the benefit of all. Within our higher nature this is our purpose. And as far as the benefit to our humanity and quality of relationships, I think this is quite obvious.

Within this practice of present moment awareness and choosing love, you will be empowered to create and maintain more satisfying and fulfilling conditions and experiences with other people. This is because you are more often engaged with your best energy. And while in this state you are recognizing the best within yourself and others. Additionally, this generates appreciation and gratitude which resonates from you, and is supportive in the creation of the future relationships and experiences that will show up as a benefit to your life.

As part of your ongoing practice, you will notice the energetic exchanges with others. How does it feel? Does the energy flow or does it feel blocked? Are you noticing negative energy from another person? If you will stay present and aware of your own energy, you will notice if you are attaching to their expressions of fear. Or are you remaining unattached to it and maintaining your peace and love? You will feel the difference.

For the sake of sharing your light and presence, you may decide to express your truth to this other person. Maybe they are unaware of their habits and communication tendencies that are negative. They may appreciate this feedback. If you choose this path, use the utmost consideration, and only do this for their benefit. Otherwise, if this person is expressing their truth, which is unsupportive to your wellness, determine the most appropriate action for you.

As you reside in this present moment awareness (without reciprocating the negative expressions of others) you can allow them to be in their energetic space while not losing your own power. This is suitable for dealing with a partner, friends, parents, children, co-workers, and even strangers, who may be temporarily expressing their lower energy.

Depending upon the situation, you will likely not always be able to maintain this level of mindfulness. That is fine, for our standard is not perfection, but evolution and ascension to a more loving state within this physical world.

Simply reconnect to your awareness as often as needed. We are working to facilitate our healing and growth, and to integrate our higher nature into our humanity. This thing called enlightened living is an on-going process, not a destination. Do your best, and always endeavor to have love and compassion for yourself.

Chapter 26
Impeccable Communication

"Whatever words we utter should be chosen with care for people will hear them and be influenced by them for good or ill."

- Buddha

In addition to our higher awareness, choosing love requires us to be accountable and honest in our communications. We must be "impeccable with our word." Don Miguel Ruiz calls this the "First Agreement" is his wonderful book, **The Four Agreements**. If we do not express our truth, then we waste precious time creating many false paths that never lead directly to love and wellness.

Regarding our current relationships, there are two things that are most important for us to uphold. First, that we know our own higher truth. This is our highest understanding at the time, which comes from our best intentions. And second, that we honor our truth by being courageous enough to express it clearly and considerately to others. Again, our expressions are intended to be supportive, we are not just blurting out our perceptions haphazardly. This is the only way to create the empowering conditions in which a relationship may thrive. And this is especially critical for the deeper connections, such as partnering or parenting.

This is our opportunity to express to another person what we want for ourselves. And as enlightened humans, what we want is always in alignment with our truth and supportive to our wellness. We would never intentionally use our communication to harm others, just as we would not want them to harm us.

Consider how often we handle our communications in an ill-advised manner. Firstly, we hesitate to express our truth, because we are undecided about what we want. Since our ego is constantly attempting to get its way, we try to anticipate all of the potential outcomes in our favor. Our communication then becomes manipulative in order to coerce the results that we think are in our best interest.

Secondly, if we are interacting regularly with someone close to us, we may expect them to somehow satisfy our needs without open communication. However, this is not their responsibility, and no one is a mind reader. And finally, we tell people what we think they want to hear, in order to avoid confrontation. But in doing so we are not honoring our truth, and this will show up later to bite us. Do not defer your problems because you are too afraid to be truthful today.

Does any of this un-impeccable communication sound familiar? How supportive do you think this is toward maintaining a healthy, happy relationship? We must be responsible for knowing our truth and then sharing our truth with conviction and kindness. Instead, in the past, we may have avoided doing this out of fear. We are afraid of being rejected, unsupported, criticized, and condemned. And our ego is not structured to handle that. In countless ways we have habitually chosen fear (ego) over love (Spirit). This is the path to suffering, from which we must awaken.

Living enlightened and honoring our truth will at times require us to be willing to be vulnerable. I know that this is a dirty word for most people. In truth our vulnerability is an indication that we need to refocus on inner healing and developing our inner strength regarding the subject at hand. It means that you are doing something that is foreign to the normal comforts of your ego. This is a good thing. Get used to it, as you awaken to your highest life you will expand into many new experiences and energetic expressions that you may have previously avoided. This is called personal growth, and it is incredibly fulfilling.

So, first and foremost, be accountable for expressing your truth. But also, be mindful in the way in which you express it. Everyone resides within their energetic space and awareness, and is primarily focused on their own needs. Be mindful and sensitive to the potential impact on another, and express your truth when and how it may be most beneficial for all involved.

Of course you cannot control or always anticipate another's response. Apply the "think before you speak" process, but also listen to your inner guidance. Sometimes our words should remain in our mind, and not spoken out loud. At other times you may have a strong inner sense that something needs to be said to someone for their benefit. So you express yourself, only to be severely admonished by this person. Sometimes there is a price to pay for speaking truth, but you have to allow the other person to hear it and deal with it in their own way. At some point they may realize the value in your expressions, but ultimately it is up to them.

When choosing love, our intention is to advance and expand positive energy for all. Otherwise, when we choose fear in any present moment, we may be more concerned with our own selfish reward, such as to be "right," approved, admired, validated, etc. Be mindful in all of your communications, and do your best to express love.

If you need to be clearer or more considerate in your speech, then attempt to clarify your comments. This can be tricky, because even if you have expressed something with only loving intent, the other person may still have misinterpreted this message in a negative way. Use your highest awareness to deal with this situation in a way that supports your truth. All we can do is allow others to be in their space of awareness (this is their truth in the present moment), and then accept them as they are.

In any case, it is your job to keep your inner peace in the moment. Accepting where their energy is aligned may be all that you can do for them. However, you always have to choose love for yourself. In certain relationships you may express your truth in as loving a manner possible, and still you are rejected by this person. Examine the circumstance, situation, and purpose of this relationship. You may decide to design a new approach of communication. Or otherwise, if they are presently relegated to unconsciousness and are generally unsupportive, you might decide to just move on. While always offering love, take the most appropriate action for you.

Regarding the forms of communication that are available to us today, choose them wisely. More often we tend to communicate with other people through text that is delivered by some device. Of course, we have new generations of people who have grown to primarily communicate in this way. I am not going to judge this as right or wrong. My only concern is that we are communicating in the most appropriate and effective fashion for a given circumstance.

Some messages are adequately delivered in a text, email, or other short social media format. You are expressing information in a concise and direct manner. Other messages are clearly better offered and received by voice conversations, whether face-to-face or over the telephone. The primary issue is that it be received in the context in which you intended. Therefore, the communication is as much about the audience or recipient as it is about you.

In my work experience as an accountant, I had some negative experiences with email. Based upon the nature of my work (and personality), my emails were designed to deliver information in a succinct way. However, at times, other people took them to be cold, short, or unfriendly. I was simply relaying information, and had no intent to express emotion at all. So because of this, I learned to send one type of email to "accounting types" and another to "marketing types." One was more direct and the other more "touchy feely." The same consideration can be made when communicating with family, friends, etc.

It seems important in these times to encourage people to talk to each other more. I understand that the time issue involved can be significant, and a quick text message is appropriate for many situations. However, the best chance to avoid misunderstanding, build relationships, and gather the most pertinent information is still often by communicating verbally. There is an aspect of human connection that is meaningful and valuable for the sake of a higher energetic connection. We definitely bring more of our presence and power into this type of communication. And this supports enlightened living.

CHAPTER 27

Be Kind, Considerate and Compassionate

"Let my soul smile through my heart and my heart smile through my eyes, that I may scatter rich smiles in sad hearts."

- Paramahansa Yogananda

Enlightened living is more common sense than rocket science or "mysterious" wisdoms. Accepting a more loving truth through greater personal accountability is not complicated, but it does require a strong interest in your inner wellness. This is about intentions and practice, not mysticism.

We all want someone to care enough to be present and available, and to share equally in our relationships. This is true regardless of the human dynamic or purpose. And we all want to be encouraged and supported, not judged and criticized. It turns out that we are all quite similar, despite our perceived differences.

The golden rule is always the best policy for enlightened living. Treat others the way you would want to be treated, right? Many things that are simple and true have not always been easy for humans. Yet, they are natural for us when we are connected to our Authentic Self. We typically treat others the way we treat ourselves in private. In other words, when we are able to offer love, kindness, and compassion to ourselves, even when WE make a mistake, we more easily express these qualities to all others. If we could see ourselves as Divine Beings simply doing the best we can within our human experience, we could transfer this higher understanding into our perceptions of others as well.

If we all were living our lives in this manner there would be no need for books like mine. This would be my paramount dream for humanity. However, the persistent self-interest of ego poisons our perceptions and separates us from our truth. So we don't trust ourselves to be unconditionally loving, kind, considerate, and compassionate. Therefore, we are unable to trust others to embody these qualities toward us. We know the fear, insecurity, hatred, and selfishness in our own mind and heart. And instead of healing and shifting to our loving truth, which takes an amount of effort and courage, we simply project our negativity out into the world.

It seems that many among us claim and express their perceived authority to determine that their way of being or believing is somehow ordained as truth for all. While those who process and function in a different way should have their rights taken away, as they are deemed unworthy of life and liberty. This human judgement is not kind, considerate, compassionate, or loving – nor is it spiritual truth. When you are healthy enough to offer your loving presence to all, you may honor your truth while accepting and appreciating the various and diverse life paths.

We who are studying and living the wisdom of enlightenment are re-connecting to our higher nature, and being more accountable to the empowerment of our relationships. It is not good enough to say that you love or like someone – and then treat them unkindly. We are surely functioning within our lower consciousness when we seek to undermine, harm, dishonor, sabotage, and ridicule others. Whether or not we are trying to do this directly, people will feel disempowered when we ignore them or are insensitive to their needs.

If you want a transcendent relationship with your partner, parents, children, or other family members, treat them with kindness, consideration, and compassion – always. If you want to develop empowering friendships or successful work relationships, be fully present, available, and offer your best energy. In order to elevate your relationships in this way, you must consistently be connected to your higher loving self – your Authentic Self. In other words, we must elevate our consciousness, leading to the higher intention and practice of choosing to express love within each present moment, and all of our relationships.

We also want to be discerning, which is a valuable attribute of being more conscious. Yet, we need to move away from being so selective about whom we are choosing to express loving energy. Our discernment keeps us alert to our state of wellness within our relationship connections, and we should listen to this awareness and act accordingly. However, when we are living in a manner that is in alignment with our higher truth, our love is more unconditional, and we seek to recognize this Divine identity within all people.

When you are unable to offer this quality of love toward others, use your awareness to recognize this temporary occurrence. This is caused by a disconnection from your higher identity. Typically, you will find that the deficit in your energy is reflecting the need to offer more love to yourself. This is why it is never selfish to prioritize self-love. It is actually the process of inner healing that then manifests as our loving presence in the world. It is the only way to facilitate loving, empowering relationships.

Learn to recognize that you are responsible for correcting this situation, others are not. If you are mentally or physically exhausted or depleted, honor your need for healing and rest. If you have temporarily attached to the negativity (fear) from another, honor your need to release this energy for the sake of healing. Create or prioritize the time and space to facilitate your own healing.

Re-connect to your Authentic Self, and remember (accept) your higher truth beyond these current circumstances. Engage in the healing steps that bring you into the power of the present moment, and shift your perceptions of yourself and others. Be patient with yourself, but be responsible for your own wellness. This will support you in maintaining transcending relationships of all kinds from the perspective of expressing the love and wellness that is your truth.

Why be kind? Kindness is the natural expression of your higher nature. No one needs to do anything to "deserve" kindness. If you are unable to express kindness to any person, you are disconnected in some way from your Authentic Self, and living in fear. It is then your responsibility, for your sake and theirs, to focus on inner healing. Our ability to be kind, especially in situations that don't directly benefit us materially, is a strong indication of whether or not we are living enlightened. By the way, gossiping, judging, and criticizing people to others are unkind and energetically harmful. Additionally, with social media we now have a communication system that is fraught with expressions based in unkindness and untruth. Elevate your energy and avoid this behavior, which is a mass demonstration of fear and unconsciousness.

Why be considerate? Consideration for others is going beyond your own needs and desires to understand how others may be affected or impacted by you. While we cannot control the response of others, our intention is always to be supportive. This is not to say that we are giving away our power or accountability for our own wellness. But in knowing that we are always empowered, we now have the capability to support the wellness of others. You may just be required to listen to them with presence. Or maybe your wisdom, advice, or service is requested. Regardless, they will feel more valued within the relationship, and more importantly, within themselves.

Why be compassionate? Compassion is an energetic expression that represents love, and it encourages Unity Consciousness. However, since it is unsupported by ego, we are required to elevate our energy and identity. With the awareness of our higher truth, we know that everyone is living their own unique path as best they can. We are all functioning within various levels of consciousness. This is just as true for your partner, parents, or children, as it is for total strangers from another part of the Earth. From our ego perspective we often cannot understand or appreciate their path, choices, or experiences, so we look upon them with fear and judgment. Compassion requires us to shift into a higher perception of their value, and offer love from this space. When we do this we are supporting them either directly or indirectly through our shared energetic foundation.

Ok, so what if another person is not kind, considerate, or compassionate to us? We all have experienced this countless times. And thus far, since I am writing this and you are reading this, it has not destroyed us yet. Still, in the moment, it does not feel very good.

Realistically, if we are present and empowered we can choose how to respond or deal with this. Otherwise, we likely lose the ability of choice, and may respond in kind out of habit. No one is benefitting from this. The goal of this book is to live enlightened within your relationships, so this seemingly unpleasant situation offers value for those who are awake.

First of all, you can hold firm in your self-love and decide not to attach your energy to their fear (ego). In that moment, if a response is appropriate, you can respond in a high-minded way. Next, you can later examine this situation to facilitate greater healing and growth. If it is supportive, ask the following questions: Why might I have attracted this negativity? Is it reflecting some negative energy or expression coming from me? Could I simply have misunderstood or misjudged the other person? What is the best course of action for maintaining my inner wellness? Is it beneficial for me to address my thoughts and feelings with this person in order to heal our relationship?

Hopefully, you recognize all of this as a superior way to function within your relationships. And while it is contrary to the typical worldly education of ego preservation and confrontation, it is highly supportive of both your spirituality and your humanity. Your expressions need not be conditional based upon the words or actions of others. To live enlightened within your relationships takes greater presence and awareness, as well as inner strength and self-love. This supports our highest purpose. And with intention, accountability, and practice it is available to you.

CHAPTER 28
Attracting Positive, Healthy Relationships

"Let there be spaces in your togetherness and let the winds of the heavens dance between you. Love one another but make not a bond of love: let it rather be a moving sea between the shores of your souls."

- Khalil Gibran

Since our relationships are energy exchange opportunities, and like energy attracts, we have a measure of control regarding the people and experiences that show up in our life. While I believe that there are some factors beyond our understanding, it is clear to me that we attract people in our life to serve some higher purpose toward inner and outer wellness.

For the sake of healing, growth, and evolution, we have a need to fill. Accordingly, we are given the opportunity to notice the reflection of our inner energetic state. When we are relatively disconnected from our higher truth and stuck in our fear-based ego perceptions we are much more likely to attract people to offer this view back to us. And while fully present and empowered we embody a state of love, joy, and peace that encourages an attraction on that level.

How we outwardly project our state of inner wellness is eminently critical to all that we manifest on the outside. It actually represents our beliefs about our self. The Divine laws of creation then work to manifest this into our physical reality. We create relationships that fulfill an energetic attraction. This may be something that develops slowly over time or more quickly. With honest self-reflection I hope that you are able to recognize this truth within your own life.

We accumulate our inner belief system based upon our early education and indoctrination into our ego culture. But also, on some level, this fits the design of our life for our specific purposes. In any case, depending upon your perception of your reality and potential, you are always creating your future. And this includes your relationship connections.

So when you are disconnected from your truth, you are attached to your ego, and may be carrying much fear. This may translate into insecurity about your worthiness or desirability as a mate, a belief in lack or poverty, or a general mistrust of others. Or you may experience some other debilitating belief caused by fear.

These beliefs become expressed as energy – as your thoughts, words, feelings, and actions. So you always attract more of what you believe in. In this case you are likely attracting what you think you don't want - the very thing that you are likely complaining about. The answer for transforming from a negative self-belief system is not to simply find the "right person" to heal, correct, or save you.

Awakening to your higher truth is an inner motivation and commitment. And it is a tool for attracting all that you want in your life. Actually, you have already been attracting the right people. It's just that they were giving evidence of your need for healing, which was unsatisfying to your ego. It always was your responsibility to be accountable for your own healing and wellness. So in truth, they did their job admirably.

Now that you know this, it's time to get busy creating and manifesting that which you DO want in your life. Think deeply about what you desire to experience. This will be unique for you, and must not simply be what others may want for you. Seek people who are supportive while you pursue your greatest dreams and vision. Focus on your own healing and wellness, as discussed throughout this book. And then establish in detail what it is that you want to create in your life.

Regarding relationships, from your healthiest energetic space you may desire to be married or single. You may desire to add new friendships or to improve the ones you have. And you may have a strong desire to be more empowered within your family relationships. According to the desires for your life, you get to choose what best honors your truth. But you will always be given the tests that require you to honor yourself first.

Your inner belief system may be transformed with love in order to create any other circumstance you want to experience. Maybe you want to start a new career or business, or get a promotion where you are now. Or you may just want to create greater satisfaction in your current job. You may want to experience greater income, or to acquire certain assets that may elevate your lifestyle. Or you may just want to experience greater appreciation and fulfillment within your current lifestyle. These topics will be discussed in future books in my *On the Enlightened Path* series.

Your transcendent relationships are created or enhanced by your expression of loving energy, and by your inner belief that you deserve to achieve your dreams. This is primarily a matter of convincing yourself, not others. Beyond your inner healing this will likely require a measure of patience. But the principles of the Law of Attraction always apply.

You will enhance this process of manifestation by intentionally shifting your mental thoughts and images to that which you desire. You must bombard your subconscious. Use affirmations and visualizations that depict you having already received. Call into existence that which you desire as if it already exists. You can acknowledge that on the level of energy it already does exist, so offer your gratitude and appreciation to Divine Source. The remainder of this process of manifesting your desire into the physical requires patience and the consistent expression of affirming energy.

Next, you must become focused and aware. Your inner guidance, or intuition, will offer many clues along the way.

More than wishing, action is usually required. You have created the mental images in as much detail as you can. Now release the concern for exactly "how and when" the thing will show up. Stay present and involved regarding any further actions you may be guided to take. This is a spiritual process which entails a higher concept of allowing the limitless potential of Divine Intelligence to work through you. Therefore, be focused on the process and non-attached to the outcome.

Beyond the principles of the Law of Attraction, be prepared to participate fully within this relationship you intend to manifest. Your presence and love is required if you are hoping for someone who will be fully loving toward you. Heal your inner wounds and release your baggage, if you want someone healthy and relatively baggage free. Learn to value and accept yourself as you are, and be prepared to do the same for the other person, if you want them to value and accept you. Take the time to understand and honor your truth, if you want to be understood and appreciated.

For what we give we receive. And what we withhold is withheld from us. If you want a positive, healthy relationship you must give positive and healthy energy. Be clear about the qualities you desire and make sure that you embody those same qualities. Transcending relationships are supportive to the higher love and wellness for each of us. So whether you want a mate, more friends, etc., be present, kind, considerate, honest, compassionate, reliable, and available.

Don't simply desire a relationship because you are being unaccountable for your own wellness. If you connect with someone from this position of fear and weakness, you will likely attract another who is riddled with a similar fear and weakness. They appear outwardly to be the answer to your prayers, because they seem to present an opportunity for things to be different in your life. And in any case, a change can sometimes feel exciting.

However, "different" quickly turns into the same familiar relationship challenges when you have not sufficiently addressed your own inner healing. And their inner doubts, fears, and negative energy are likely as compelling as yours. This will come out eventually. And with any level of awareness you will realize that they are not capable of solving your inner needs. Only you can do this yourself.

If you are hoping to attract a spouse, with the intention of happily-ever-after, you must be able to understand and know within yourself what this actually looks like to you. While connected to your Authentic Self, what is truth for you? It takes more than an initial physical attraction and some likable qualities. The deeper issues of compatibility of desires and goals must be honestly addressed. Remember, you are intending to manifest an empowered marriage, and not a temporary learning experience. While there should be ongoing growth and evolution for each of you, a proper examination of your individual desires and qualities of wellness must be determined.

Enlightenment within your relationships entails both, practical accountability and spiritual law. Develop your level of inner healing in order to express your best energy for yourself and all others. You therefore, will attract another who is similarly focused upon their own wellness. And then through your impeccable communications and sharing of loving energy you may determine the true purpose and potential of the relationship. How does this connection affect your energy on the level of Spirit? And how does it satisfy and fulfill your human desires in partnership?

Once fully engaged in an empowered relationship, continue to maintain your own inner wellness. Your ongoing connection to your higher self will facilitate the greatest support of your partner. Love, honor, and encourage them, while allowing and accepting them as they are. You chose them through your highest consciousness, so don't start trying to control or change them now.

Live in a state elevated from fear as often as possible. Be empowered to work together to solve the human issues that come up in your daily life. Focus on ways to serve yourself, each other, and the world. This creates lives of meaning that are more expansive than the little ego challenges that may arise.

I wish you well on your unique journey to create many transcending relationships. May you find and connect to your Authentic Self, as you facilitate your own healing, growth, and evolution. May you develop your inner wellness so as to express your loving presence to all of those in your life. And may you transform your life toward embracing Unity Consciousness for the betterment of all life on the planet.

PART III: Exercises

1) Evaluate your current partner relationship. If you are not in a committed intimate relationship at this time, consider your close friends. In your private space, make the effort to become aware of the primary energy between you. Is it dominated by fear (anger, frustration, negativity, stress, disappointment, judgement, resentment, shame, etc.)? Or is it predominately based in love (joy, peace, support, consideration, respect, patience, etc.)?

2) Now, in full accountability and honesty, look within yourself to recognize how and why you are creating these conditions through attraction. This is not about your partner, it is about you. What is it about your energetic expressions that facilitate the dynamic between you? How does this reflect your inner need for healing from past relationships or from a false and disempowering self-image?

3) What steps may you take toward fully honoring your Authentic Self and elevating your relationships and connection to all people? Do you need to be more accountable for your own wellness and happiness? Do you need to be more accepting of the other person's truth? Do you need to shift your perception of yourself or them? Do you need to find greater appreciation for yourself or others? Do you need to express and communicate your truth more freely, honestly, or effectively? If you answer yes to any of these, search within for the specific steps or actions needed.

PART III: Affirmations

I AM now offering my loving Presence within my relationships.

I AM now connected to my Authentic Self as I share my Presence.

I AM now offering my loving Presence to my partner (spouse).

I AM now offering my loving Presence to my children.

I AM now valuing and accepting myself and all others.

I AM now taking responsibility for all of my relationships.

I AM now expressing my truth within all of my relationships.

I AM now honoring myself within all of my relationships.

I AM now embracing Unity Consciousness in support of all life.

I AM now healing within and attracting healthy relationships.

I AM now empowered to create Transcending Relationships.

ABOUT THE AUTHOR

Scott E. Clark brings his own practical life experience and inner guidance into his writing. He has learned valuable life lessons leading to his own ongoing transformational development. Some of his roles, titles, relationships, and responsibilities, include son, father, grandfather, husband, friend, employee, business owner, student, teacher, and author.

His highest intention with his writing and teaching is to offer a philosophy and path that may guide others to recognize their true potential through wisdom, mindfulness and personal accountability. This is attained through inner healing and growth, and then expressed out into the world. Even while spending 30 years in the corporate world, primarily in accounting management, his passion introduced him to the higher principles and possibilities of life.

His foundation in spiritual understanding is to include and accept all people as equal spiritual beings who are each on their own unique path of consciousness and evolution. It is from this perspective and energy that he has written, *"On the Enlightened Path"*, as the inspired message he has been guided to share. His natural inclination toward balance, logic, and practicality serves his purpose of introducing the integration of spiritual principles into everyday life.

The titles in his *"On the Enlightened Path"* book series are: *Mastering Your Life; Transcending Relationships; Career Success; Holistic Wellness*; and *Conscious Parenting*. Mr. Clark is also the author of, *"The Empower Model for Men: a guide to more conscious living"*, published in 2014.

Mr. Clark recognizes that there are many road maps to higher wisdom and inspiration, and for each of us it is a matter of finding our own path of truth. Some examples of the various ancient and contemporary books and wisdom teachings that have inspired him on his journey are: Buddhism, A Course in Miracles, Kriya Yoga, Tao Te Ching, The Bhagavad Gita, The Yoga Sutras, The Power of Now, The Four Agreements, The Law of Attraction, and many more.

After his extensive professional business career, as an accountant and financial manager and CPA, he now serves as an author, teacher, and mentor in the field of personal and spiritual growth and development. Mr. Clark resides in sunny Phoenix, Arizona, and engages in a daily meditation practice and fitness routine in support of his own holistic wellness. As he continues to fulfill his higher purpose in service to the world, he cherishes time with his children, grandchildren, family, and friends.